# JACK CHURCHILL
*"Unlimited Boldness"*

An Anthology of the exploits of a very brave warrior

Copyright © Oxon Publishing Ltd 2015

ISBN 978-1-870677-06-6

All rights reserved. Without limiting the rights under copyright reserved above, no part of this publication may be reproduced, stored in or introduced into a retrieval system, or transmitted, in any form or by any means (electronic, mechanical, photocopying, recording or otherwise), without the prior written permission of both the copyright owner and the above publisher of this book

Printed and bound by CPI Group (UK) Ltd, Croydon, CR40 4YY

Photographs and illustrations are facsimiles taken from the original publications courtesy of the Churchill family

Cover design by Temple Design Publishing Solutions Ltd:
Cover image by Arabella Dorman

# ACKNOWLEDGEMENTS

Mrs Jean King-Clark has enthusiastically supported the idea of this Anthology and kindly granted copyright to the publisher.

The book has been edited and published by Robert Forsyth under his own imprint, *Oxon Publishing Ltd*. Robert lives in Deddington where the Churchill family lived for several hundred years until the early 20$^{th}$ Century. Robert has placed the family's history on the parish website at:
www.deddington.org.uk/history/people/thechurchillsofdeddington

Such modest profits that arise from the sale of the book will be donated to the Manchester Regiment's Museum in Ashton-under-Lyme and to Friends of Deddington Library where Rex's books and various histories of the Churchill family can be obtained.

*Free for a Blast* (Grenville Publishing) and *Jack Churchill 'Unlimited Boldness'* (Fleur-de-Lys Publishing) are now both out of print. Every effort has been made to contact the publishers but without success. Their contributions to the original publications are hereby acknowledged: in particular, the Title page image, Dryden's quote on page 33 and the obverse side Dedication and Contents are reproduced from the cover and introductory pages created by Fleur-de-Lys Publishing.

The text of this publication is taken verbatim from the original books without any copy editing. Any idiosyncrasies by today's standards of spelling or punctuation therefore remain.

# FOREWORD

...ne: A commuter train is about a mile short of its destination of ...miles out of London. Five home-going London city workers look ...ent as one of their number, who has been poring over documents in ...ng Ministry of Defence briefcase, gets up from his seat, opens the ...is briefcase out into the night, closes the window and regains his ...n appalled and astonished silence. No one knows that this is the ...ne Colonel "Mad Jack" Churchill, and he is simply depositing his ...arge back garden to lighten his load on his walk home from the

...of writings about one of the bravest soldiers of WWII by his friend ...ier, Rex King-Clark, covers the remarkable life of the last British ...n enemy soldier with a bow and arrow - during the Dunkirk retreat ...larly entered into commando combat armed with bagpipes and a ...is a revolver and his longbow.

...g covers an adventure filled trip that Jack and Rex took across ... as recounted in Chapter Two of *Free for a Blast;* this allows the ...p an understanding of what made Jack Churchill "tick".

...y the re-publication of his military biography of Jack, published ...r of *'Unlimited Boldness'*.

...in 1944 on a Yugoslav island, because of his name, Jack was flown ...nterred in the notorious Sachsenhausen concentration camp with ...ers such as Von Thyssen and Schacht, but, dissatisfied with camp ...accommodation, he tunnelled out of the camp with a well known ...immie James. He was recaptured and, sometime later, transferred to ...n the Tyrol, from which he escaped yet again and finally reached ...ere met up with an American Column having travelled for several ...mely mountainous and rugged country.

...is my personal tribute to a very brave man whose reputation and ...have long admired.

---

Correction to FOREWORD

Jack Churchill met up with the American column in Italy and not in Switzerland

# CONTENTS

FREE FOR A BLAST     1
Chapter 2 - Grand Tour


UNLIMITED BOLDNESS     33


POST SCRIPTS     55

# FREE FOR A BLAST

## CHAPTER TWO - GRAND TOUR

Rex King-Clark
from a painting executed by Leslie W Lang RBA in Capri 1936

# GRAND TOUR

THE YEAR 1936 was, I suppose, the most memorable of my life. It brought increased interest in my vocation as a soldier and, in other fields, provided excitement, tragedy and, finally, comedy.

With the aid of my small platoon of fifteen-or-so NCOs and men, during my third year in the 2nd Manchesters I at last began to learn, during training and everyday regimental life, the responsibilities of command and leadership. These included coming to terms not only with straight spoken solid men of Lancashire but also with volatile Welshmen and Irishmen, both well represented in the Manchesters as in many Regiments recruited in the north-west.

The last, with the Irish contrariness, supplied the Regiment with many excellent warrant officers and NCOs, leavened with some of our harder cases. My platoon sergeant, Kirwan, and one of my section corporals, Nolan, represented the former group while Private "Kelly" represented the latter. The fact that up till joining the Battalion I had never met any of these "ethnic groups" - my life having been spent in Scotland or Southern England - kept me alert and made my soldiering more intriguing.

Sport alongside work has always been a tradition in the British Army. In this I was fortunate since I was "quite good at games" - an inherited bonus for which I claim no kudos. I could play alongside the soldiers of the Battalion in soccer, rugger, cricket and hockey and later, abroad, could swim and play water polo with them.

As an aside, in India, in 1942, I achieved some small fame in the 2nd Infantry Division Scotland vs. England soccer match by scoring the only goal of the match direct from a corner kick. It curled low into the English net without touching anyone: A sheer fluke which prompted much touchline whistling from the Jocks of the Royal Scots and Camerons.

Our off duty life as subalterns followed a pretty normal "young man" pattern, with some built-in Sandhurst disciplines. In plain clothes, for instance, we always wore a hat or cap when out-of-doors

We formed friendships with those with common interests, in my case Martin Bury, my contemporary and St Mary's partner and Jack Churchill. He was five years my senior in terms of service and experience of life. Later, when Jack temporarily left the Army, I became friends with Henry Frisby, a couple of years my junior.

"Common interests" in the case of Jack were mainly concerned with motoring and motorbikes, the latter his lifetime passion[1]. With Henry it was flying. We took our A licences together at York and subsequently flew together many times in the Club Gipsy I Moths in inter-club "dawn patrols". We aerobatted together - including illegal flick half-rolls which, with the lap strap over one shoulder, Bill Humble taught us, and competed against each other in the number of spin turns we could make before our nerve failed. Of course, these antics were carried out well away from the aerodrome and the watchful eye of Tony Pick, our flying instructor.

As well as motoring and flying with both Jack and Henry, we visited many fine pubs in and around York, drinking endless pints of mild and bitter, especially at Harry

---

[1] See *Jack Churchill - Unlimited Boldness*" - Military Chest Magasine, March-June 1985 (Picton Publishing).

Smith's Star Inn in Stonegate. Here one drew one's own pint and put the money in the till in between playing dominoes and darts with local regulars.

Our evening excursions to pubs, occasional dances (normally in white tie and tails) or on dates were limited by mandatory dining-in nights (mess kit, except at weekends when a black tie sufficed) in the old, Great War vintage, wooden mess building, similar to the huts in which the dozen or so unmarried officers of the battalion were quartered. These excursions usually tailed off towards the end of the month owing to lack of funds and imminent mess bills

Sometimes extended periods as orderly officer were imposed by the adjutant on erring subalterns, which further limited extra-curricular activity. My longest period of incarceration was a fortnight. I had, without leave, left the station to drive to London and was late on parade on Monday morning. I had stopped the car in Newark and fallen asleep, to be woken, too late, by a polite policeman.

In spite of, or perhaps because of these restrictions we were generally a happy bunch at Strensall Camp, York, with a good corporate sense of humour and, necessarily, of the ridiculous.

In the spring of 1936 I bought a J4 MG. During that summer, I raced it in as many events as I could squeeze in between bouts of company and battalion training on Strensall Common, at Ripon and on the Yorkshire Moors.

As I have also recounted, in August 1936 I bought my first aeroplane, a Miles Hawk (G-ACTD). On the last day of that month, a Sunday, with Henry Frisby as passenger in the front seat, I crashed her while landing at Doncaster.

In mid-September 1936 I returned to the Battalion from hospital with nothing worse than a broken nose, a vivid scar from my right nostril to the corner of my mouth - giving me a semi-permanent leer on that side—and a bruised behind. It was less than I deserved after such a severe accident, which had been no one's fault but mine.

A few days later, on 26th September 1936, Eric Costin, my CO, sent for me. Looking at me directly, but with understanding as he always did, he told me that Henry had died of his injuries. I had been anticipating this with dread for some while, for Henry had remained unconscious since the crash with severe head and spine injuries. Afterwards everyone was considerate and sympathetic (which confused me), for while I felt guilt, I felt no real grief - just a mental numbness which may have been the aftermath of the concussion and shock resulting from the accident.

There followed Henry's funeral at the lovely little church in his home village of Bacton in Herefordshire. His parents were very kind and I met, for the first time, his brother Dick, an officer in The Royal Hampshire Regiment, who later distinguished himself as a leader in the war that was to come. It was the first time I had met any of Henry's family and, even in my low state, I recognised their quality. In retrospect, I am sure that Henry, had he lived, would have maintained the high standard set by them - both as a man and a soldier. He was certainly no stranger to courage or initiative. I was to miss him greatly as a friend and companion.

The next hurdle was the Coroner's inquest at which the finding was "accidental death." The accident officer from the Air Ministry gave evidence to the effect that there had been no negligence, a finding which gave me relief, but only confused me further, since it was my piloting error which had caused the accident. When all this was over, I had to go before a War Office medical board at York Hospital, after which I was told to go away on three months sick leave, with a further medical board to follow at the end it.

Three months' leave! Whatever was I going to do with it? Having no home base and since my elder sister, married to Spencer Maclure of the 60th Rifles, was out in Burma with their 1st Battalion, my thoughts turned automatically to The Hollies in Kirn. I decided to inflict myself on my Aunties Janey and Nellie for a few days as a starter. However, there was one appointment to be kept first and that was the Yorkshire Sports Car Club Speed Trials at the end of the month at Wetherby. These speed trials were held on a stretch of slightly uphill road with an early bend - and with an uncertain surface - in the park of Wetherby Grange, the home of Sir Ronald Gunter Bt. Sir Ronald, the instigator of these trials, himself a well-known racing motorist and car enthusiast, had bought a Type 540 K Mercedes-Benz at the 1934 London Motor Show to add to his stable. In the ring of 1935 he had invited a friend and myself over to the Grange to see this magnificent machine. It was truly the car to end all cars.

Looking back, I must have been crazy to have even considered taking part in the Wetherby event, since I was still far from well. One cannot tell, but perhaps it was due to an innate desire to prove to myself - and to others - that nothing had changed - that everything was back to normal - which, of course, it wasn't.

On the day, Paddy Gray, my soldier servant, and I were driven over to Wetherby by a friend in his Rover and I can remember, with shame, raving at Paddy the whole day, when I discovered my helmet and goggles were not in the car - which was not his responsibility anyway. It was grossly unfair of me, but Paddy never said a word.

The MG was already waiting for us at the course with a little crowd round her, having been taken over on a trailer by the City Garage of York. On form, I should have won the two classes for which we were entered and have come third overall. In the event, I made a nonsense of the whole thing, thoroughly frightened myself - though no doubt exciting the 2,500 spectators - when, on both runs, I went off the road onto the grass at the gentle left-hand bend a hundred yards or so from the start, while still accelerating hard in second gear. Both times I drove back onto the road and finished, but only managed second place in one class, the 850 cc S/1100 cc un-supercharged category - with a time of 32.87 sec for the standing start half-mile and fourth overall.

Cummings, driving his supercharged Vauxhall Villiers in the open class made the fastest time of the day in 30.20 sec but, as the Light Car reported, "swerved onto the grass verge when seventy yards past the finishing line and, after another fifty yards, collided with a tree, rebounding three times into the roadway. Although Cummings was entirely uninjured his car was a total wreck." In my diary I wrote, with some truth, "the course is too narrow and rather dangerous - and there is not much room to stop at the end."

The driving, for me, had, in fact, felt wrong from the beginning. As I had settled - with my legs astride the prop-shaft housing - into the narrow cockpit, felt the wheel trembling in my hands as I blipped the engine, sniffed the burning Castrol 'R' and looked over the little screen along the slender bonnet to the bare, front tires, I had waited for the old magic feeling of unity to settle over us. But it didn't; instead I felt separate and irritable and, at the same time, reckless. And that's how I drove. Throughout and afterwards, the taste of that day was of flat champagne.

I suppose somebody should have told me not to be such a bloody young fool and to convalesce for a while - but who, at twenty-three, listens to advice anyway?

Since I knew that Jack Churchill, who had resigned his commission at the beginning of 1936 after ten years' service was at a loose end at that time, his business

..ture not having prospered[1], invited him to come with me to Scotland - and maybe beyond.

He jumped at this and a few days later I went down to York station to meet him. Exactly on time, the train, hauled still by one of Gresley's shiny, green LNER 4-6-2 Pacifics, having averaged 70 mph from King's Cross, hissed to a gentle halt at the platform. A moment later a carriage door opened and out stepped Jack, pale hair gleaming, moustache out-brushed, suitcase in one hand, black doodle-sack in the other. He spotted me, his white teeth gleamed in a broad grin and he walked towards me with that built-in swagger, as if a pipe march was forever sounding in his ears.

After the briefest of greetings - "Hello Jack" - "Hello Clark" - we were away to Strensall for the night, in the new MG 2-litre of which I had just taken delivery and which I have described in the Introduction. The next day the two 'squatters' (Jack and I were of identical build - of medium height and a trifle solid; it was Jack's term for the pair of us) set off up the A1. Our first brief stop was at the Scottish border for a short piping and dancing session at the roadside, to the astonished double-takes of the rare passing motorist[2].We drove through Musselburgh -'The Honest Toun' - without stopping as Cuffy, my brother, had left Loretto the previous summer and was spending a year at school near Blois, in France, learning the language and enjoying life with his stable of ancient French motor-bikes. Beyond that his horizon was still obscured, though matters mechanical, coupled with a military style of life, loomed through the haze as an attractive prospect.

In the event, Cuffy took a short service commission in the Royal Air Force in 1937. He spent the early months of the war in Coastal Command - based at Dyce, near Aberdeen, flying anti-submarine patrols in Tiger Moths over the North Sea -with a basket of carrier pigeons in the front cockpit as the sole means of communication with his base[3]. In 1940, when he was twenty-two, he was transferred to 23 Squadron - armed with Blenheim night fighters - at Wittering in Huntingdonshire. On the night of 18th June he was shot down and killed over Newmarket - either by return fire from the Heinkel III they were attacking or by 'friendly' anti-aircraft fire. This was the squadron's first sortie in its night fighter role - "when three enemy aircraft were destroyed for the loss of one Blenheim[4]."

In one of the last letters my brother wrote me, he said, "This war makes one feel and act entirely on impulses. You've got to keep a grip on yourself, especially in this (night fighting) job."

Cuffy, Henry, Jack - and myself - belonged, I believe, to that section of our generation (surely a sound generation on the whole, if less stable than our fathers') which managed, somehow, to be frivolous and high-minded at the same time.

From Edinburgh, where we had stayed the night, Jack and I drove over to Helensburgh where Jean, my younger sister, lived at that time. We stayed the night at

---

[1] Jack: "You can say that again! In fact the venture went down not the drain but the Bay of Biscay."
[2] I had, somehow, been included in the Loretto team that won the Highland Fling foursome at the Scottish Public Schools OTC Camp at Elie, in Fife, in 1931. The following year I flunked the solo sword dance by forgetting my steps half-way through - although we had practised for months under the great Willie Ross. A complete mental black - out, embarrassing to one and all.
[3] Of No. 1 Coastal Patrol Flight formed from 612 Squadron RAF.
[4] *Fighter Squadrons of the RAF and their Aircraft* by John Rawlings (Macdonald 1961).

the Queen's Hotel, once the home of Henry Bell, who built and operated the first steamship, *The Comet*. The following morning, leaving Jack behind, I set out in the Big MG for my sister's house, dressed, unconventionally in slacks and sweater. (No hacking jacket, regimental tie and cap; thank God the senior subaltern couldn't see me). At the hotel entrance I stopped to offer an old lady, whom I had seen in the small conservatory lounge the previous night, a lift into the town, which she accepted. Having settled into the seat beside me she opened the conversation by asking if I were the boot-boy at the hotel. To my shame, instead of saying 'Yes' and saving her embarrassment, I said, "No, I'm not: I'm staying at the hotel", thereby covering her with confusion. She tried to put her gaffe right by saying, "Oh! I'm sorry - I must introduce you to my daughter tonight." However, we left during that day so I never discovered what delights I had missed.

From Helensburgh - both now clad in the kilt - we drove through Whistlefield, stopping at the crest to acknowledge, with a small piece on the pipes, the vista over Loch Goil - "the second best view on Scotland". Then on we careered, round the head of Loch Long into Argyll, and up the narrow serpentine road leading to the summit of 'Rest and be Thankful', where, overlooked from the East by the abrupt, eroded flanks of Ben Arthur, more piping and leaping about were insisted upon by Jack.

A detour off the road to Kirn was then taken in search of the Sweet Maid of Glendaruel, whom we finally tracked down - or one of them ('freckles and all', I see from my diary) - in the garden of a wayside croft. With some diffidence, she allowed Jack to serenade her as she stood, tousle-haired by the hedge, with the pipe tune of that name. That item ticked off the agenda, we turned back and sped along the shore road of the steep, be-shadowed Lock Eck to Kirn, to *'The Hollies' to* the Aunts and to the stern-faced but warm-hearted Forbes - the archetypal 'old retainer' - under whose eagle eye I had learned, over the years, unfailingly to wipe my shoes thoroughly on the front door mat, whether entering or leaving the house.

The pleasure at seeing my dear aunts again was equalled by the joy at once again being at *The Hollies,* which - my parents both having died - was now 'home' to me more than anywhere else.

The house itself, by far the oldest on the shore road, lies halfway between Kirn and Dunoon Piers. It looks straight across the Clyde to the Cloch Lighthouse on the Renfrewshire shore, a mile and three-quarters distant. Originally it had been two smaller houses, which the Society of Fishermen had bought in the 18th Century and knocked into one as a Home for their elderly members. They had named it *'Society House'*. That the union of the two houses had been effected in a fairly simple fashion was evident from the fact that the upstairs passage from the study to the drawing room ran steeply uphill[1].

However, the climb was well worth it, for the view from the drawing room window was magnificent.

In a letter I have before me, written on 20 March 1844 by my great-grandfather, James Clark, (who had bought *Society House* in 1828 and renamed it *The Hollies)* to

---

[1] Many years later, I was walking along the upstairs passage of the Horse Guards in Whitehall, which also runs steeply uphill, with Brigadier Gerry Duke of the Royal Engineers (later Engineer-in-Chief - a great man with a wonderful wit), and I said to him, "This building looks as if it were designed by a sapper - sir!" "You're wrong, Rex", he replied, "It was designed by two sappers."

..ı Caldwell, a Paisley friend, a weaver,[1] who tired of the mills, had emigrated with nis wife to Canada in about 1820, he says: "I have a House at Dunoon which commands the most extensive views you ever saw from my window.

"I can see Helensburgh, Gourock, Loch Long, Holly (sic) Loch, Clough (Cloch) Lighthouse, which is right opposite my House, the point which leads into Largs, which I call quarter point, Knock Hill, Hunterston, big and wee Combray (Cumbrae) with its lighthouse, Ailsa Rock, Lamlash Island, Gourock (Garroch) Head, Toward Point leading into Rothsay, with a fine view of the village of Dunoon about three-quarters of a mile from me.

"My garden is fine rising ground at the back of my House containing a full scotch lawn with a fine wall and stocked with fruit trees and bushes. Now Sir I can leave this any day and get to Paisley in one hour and thirty five minutes (by steamer and rail) all for 6d."

My great grandfather, God bless him, was laying it on a bit - but it is still a fine panorama. In the same letter (in which he refers to his friend as "living in the wilds of America", whereas in truth he was living on a fine farm at Trout River, Hinchinbrook, in Lower Canada near the St. Lawrence River) he waxes lyrical, not only about " 13,000 spindls driven by a 50 Horse and a 25 Horse power Engins" (sic) at his Paisley mill, but also over employing the "200 finest looking young Lassies as ever you saw in Paisley, which is saying a great deal and the fack (sic) is I am proud to show them when strangers happen to call and many are the times I have been told even by Americans who have visited us that there appearance was an honour to our work." (Why 'even by Americans'?)

However, John Caldwell would not have been envious. In writing, in September 1826, of the farm he was building up, he had said, "I have bid a long farewell to the four posts of misery - the loom." In fact, by 1848 James Clark was receiving letters from friends expressing envy of John Caldwell. One, John Crawford, wrote from Largs," I must say that our old friend Caldwell with his 100 acres in America might have condescended to notice me (in his letter) a little more particularly than he did, but let this pass."

But back to *The Hollies:*

In the corner of the bay window in the upstairs drawing room was the huge brass Dollond telescope on its wooden tripod stand. It was powerful enough, some years earlier, to have enabled my Aunt Janey to spot, on the road near the Cloch Lighthouse, nearly two miles away, a carter unmercifully whipping his horse. She was so outraged that she telephoned the police station in Gourock - to the carter's subsequent surprise. As boys on holiday, the telescope was a great attraction to my brother, Cuffy, and myself and we would examine every detail of the ships as they passed up or down river - HM vessels; Anchor, Canadian Pacific and Cunard liners; cargo vessels, dredgers and yachts large and small. Occasionally we were plucked from our beds to view, sleepily, a pale spotted, full moon that filled the lens.

---

[1] At that time, the Paisley weaver was his own master. "He came and went at his convenience", an old account says. "When he took a day's pleasure - fishing, curling, bowling or berrying - he made up for it before or after as pleased him. The loom was his own property and he was answerable to his employer only." The population of Paisley in 1818 was 34,800 of which between 6,000 and 7,000 were weavers.

Henry - in an unusually pensive mood

The Austin 12 at the Hollies - Aunt Janey at the door - Aunt Nellie at the wheel

The big MG being hoisted aboard the Dover-Calais Packet - 26th October 1936

Immediately across the road from the house and tucked under the railings of the ...enade, was Sand's Boating and Bathing Station - another great attraction when we were small. Here, in cubicles cut into the rock under the road, one could change into one's bathing dress and take a dip in the forbiddingly cold, but crystal clear waters of the Firth of Clyde - or, if one preferred and could afford it, hire a well-made little clinker-built dinghy for a row or to fish for saithe, codling or whiting with a handline and mussels for bait. Or, in high summer, to troll for mackerel round the rocky Gantocks off Dunoon Pier.

My two aunts were classical spinsters and absolute dears. Janey, the elder, aged seventy-seven, was the stronger character. One could, indeed, sense this in her somewhat thin face, definite cheek bones and high-bridged nose. Nellie, at sixty-three, the youngest of the family of eight, with traces of ginger still in her hair, was the adventurous one. She had been a good golfer and a skilled helmswoman in Clyde 19/24 and International Six Metre class yachts in the 1920's and 30's.

Nellie also drove the family car, a ponderous Austin 12 Landaulet, with a massive gate-gear change and a terminal velocity of 46mph[1]. Before the death of their father and mother, Robert and Ellen Clark (the former in 1928 at the age of 95, the latter in 1925 aged 87), the family had lived, during the winters, at their London home at 255 Cromwell Road, on the corner of Earls Court Road, moving to *The Hollies* each summer. Nellie and Janey would take the car up, while the rest travelled by train. Once, my sister, Jean, accompanied the Aunts. The journey took four days, Nellie driving all the way. Every two or three hours, at a suitable vantage point, Janey would say, "Nellie, you may stop and take your smoke." The car would stop, Nellie would climb out and light her cigarette; the other two would sit in the car and admire the view, with the cumbersome rear hood up or down according to the weather. The last 'five minute smoke' was taken at the top of 'Rest and Be Thankful,' the final and formidable hurdle of the journey North for the pedestrian Austin - but which had proved no problem to our fleet MG.

My aunts had been concerned to hear of my accident and were relieved when they discovered there was not much wrong with me. After all, though there were plenty of Clark descendants on the distaff side - Stoops, Bevingtons and so on - the male line was very thin on the ground - just my brother and myself. It was to grow even thinner within a few years.

Sadly *The Hollies* eventually had to be sold after the death of my Auntie Nellie. My wife, our young son and daughter, our bull terrier and I, in the summer of 1954, travelled north from Lancashire, where we were awaiting my Battalion's move to Berlin, to sort out the old house. We arrived, late in the day, to be greeted by a solemn Forbes, who, though her future had been well looked after, was naturally upset to be leaving after so many years with the family.

Having ensured that all of us, including Toughie, the bull terrier, had properly wiped their feet on the front door mat, I enquired if there was any refreshment available after the long drive. Forbes, understanding the Scottish connotation, said that, though the Misses Clark had not taken drink, she believed there might be something in the bottom right cupboard of the sideboard in the dining room. I looked and - and there it

---

[1] This was achieved on 8th August 1931 on the shore road between Kirn and Dunoon piers, while racing to catch the steamer to Queen's Pier, Greenock, where RMS Antonia was waiting to take me to Canada.

was: a squat, three-quarter full bottle of Martell cognac -purely medicinal - and three half bottles of 1898 - yes, 1898! - Champagne - Giesler & Co. of Avize, near Rheims - relics, perhaps, of some long forgotten celebration. The cognac proved to be very good; the champagne was undrinkable, though my wife Jean and I tried hard.

A local man subsequently bought *The Hollies* and he converted it into two flats. When last in Kirn I heard that the drawing room-half of the house was occupied by a United States Navy Captain and his family - no doubt from 'the wilds of America' He was based at the USN Polaris submarine depot ship in the Holy Loch, three miles northward along the shore from Kirn. The Captain was well placed, as long as he had a decent telescope, to keep an eye on his huge charges as they made their sinister way down the Firth to patrol duties in the Atlantic and beyond.

During our drive North, Jack and I had decided to extend our trip to Scotland by taking in France and, possibly, Italy as well. This may seem to readers a roundabout route to follow, but it was, however, fairly in line with the way our somewhat impulsive thought-processes worked at that time. It also fitted in with the final Brooklands meeting of 1936 (on 17th October) for which I was entered, although I hadn't dared to tell the Aunts of this. Perhaps, like Wetherby, I should, have cancelled, but I could foresee that, with my foreign posting looming up, it might be my last ever motor race - as indeed it proved to be, and, moreover, after a week with Jack how could I fail already to be feeling, physically and mentally, much better.

However, before returning south we still had one pleasant commitment ahead of us - an invitation to stay a few days with the Berrys at *Glenstriven,* before they returned to their winter quarters in North Berwick. *Glenstriven,* a traditional-style Victorian shooting lodge, lay high on the hillside, midway along the eastern shore of Loch Striven, a remote Firth of Clyde sea loch that runs deep into the hills between Loch Fyne and Loch Long[1]. The house was approached by the shore road from Dunoon, through Inellan, Toward and, finally, Inverchaolain (pronounced, needless to say, Inverhoolin) which ended in the gravel sweep at *Glenstriven's* front door steps. At the small lodge at the entrance to the estate, a minor road forked left down to the pier and its cottage.

The *Glenstriven* estate extended to some 2,000 acres of hill, moor and peat bog, with *Cruach Nan Capull,* at over 2,000 feet, about a mile inland of the house, the whole bisected by the Invervegain Burn, the mouth of which lay not far from the pier. Behind the house was the home farm, whose blackface sheep bespeckled in white, the bare green hillsides above. The home policy, enclosing the entrance lodge, the main house, the farmhouse, the pier and the lower pools of the burn, was thickly wooded with a remarkable variety of trees. From the house - a long, one-storey grey stone building - one viewed beyond the front lawns, over the tops of the trees, across the loch, the steep bracken and heatherclad hills of the far shore, on which there were neither roads, tracks nor - save for a ruined croft on the shore - any buildings, and where only an occasional shepherd ever set foot - or sets foot, I hope, to this day.

*Glenstriven's* magic lay in its utter peace, which overlay it like a soft, warm blanket, and in its simple, slow, though quite formal pattern of life.

Walter Berry I had first met at Loretto, when I was a boy of 14 or so and he was

---

[1] "Not popular with yachts", the Clyde Cruising Club Sailing Instructions say, adding, "The winds are baffling and, at times, the squalls (off the hills) are very fierce and erratic" and "mostly the soundings are deep right up to the shore."

ɪnor of the school. Through the good offices of my cousin and guardian, 'Uncle .ce Clark, who was also a Governor, Walter Berry invited me to stay during one ɔummer holidays. I enjoyed myself so much that, thereafter, it became an annual event - latterly for both my brother, Cuffy, and myself.

The household at *Glenstriven,* during the summer occupation, consisted of Walter Berry himself, his sister, Miss Anne Berry, and a cook and housemaid whose names, though we became good friends, I'm ashamed to say I have forgotten. Throughout the year a couple lived in the entrance lodge and, in the pier cottage, stayed old Macfarlane and his wife. Miss Berry, who must have been in her seventies when I knew her, was the chatelaine. She was kind, disciplined and efficient - like my Auntie Janey! She was also a keen amateur photographer, using a large, elaborate, half-plate camera, which she set up on a tripod before use. Furthermore, she did her own developing and printing.

Walter Berry, a bachelor, was of the now virtually extinct 'type Edwardian'. Born in 1863, he was in his mid-sixties when I first visited *Glenstriven* and still a fine-looking man. Though suffering from severe arthritis in his legs, he never conceded to disability. To my dismay, each morning he would stump, with his sticks, down the

*Jack & RKC at Glenstriven
(Photograph by Miss Anne Berry - 1936)*

*RKC with record trout (12oz) from the
Invervegain Burn 1931
(Photograph by Miss Anne Berry - 1931)*

corridor past my bedroom to the bathroom. Ten minutes later I would hear him returning down the passage as I lay curled up in my warm bed. I would hear him stop, there would be a 'tap-tap' on the door with his stick, "Robert - good morning - your bath is ready.""My bath", I knew, meant a foot of ice-cold, brown peaty water - into which he had already plunged, arthritis and all, keeping up the Spartan habit he had learned at Loretto nearly half a century before, which I had had to follow but had always deplored.

In his youth, Walter had been a remarkable athlete. From Loretto, where, as a cricketer, in five 1st XI inter-school matches between 1879 and 1882, he had taken 35 wickets for 46 runs and played for the 1st XV for two seasons, he had gone up to Oxford where he had gained a Rugger Blue, followed by being capped for Scotland.

He had inherited wealth. I don't believe he ever 'worked', though in his lifetime he did a great deal of good, especially for young people and for his dependants. He died in 1947 at the age of 84, a much-loved man. In his will he left me a tortoiseshell cigarette case, though I did not need anything to remind me of his kindness or of the magic of *Glenstriven*.

My other particular friend at *Glenstriven* was old Macfarlane. He had, originally, been the estate fisherman, keeping the community supplied with herring netted from the shoals which filled the loch each season. However, the herring, over the years, had largely disappeared from the Clyde[1] and Macfarlane had become a kind of general factotum around the estate. He and his wife were Highland gentlefolk - calm, perfectly mannered, bi-lingual in Gaelic and sibilant English and with a subtle sense of humour - though in Macfarlane's case this last could sometimes be expressed in a disconcerting manner.

I recall one evening, when he and I were out in the launch fishing for mackerel, the inboard-engine had given up the ghost and refused to be restarted. After cranking away for some minutes without success, while I was blethering away with advice and other nonsense, Macfarlane turned to me and said politely, "It may be the electrissity, Robert. Will you chust be holding these two wires and letting me know if you feel anything when I turn the flywheel."

Obediently I took hold of the leads, he wound hard on the starting handle and the shock threw me backwards into the bottom of the boat. As I climbed shakily to my feet, he murmured, "Well, it can't be the electrissity, that iss for sure."

Macfarlane had another claim to fame in my eyes as a boy: he wore a red wig under his tweed cap. Perhaps the colour was a small concession to vanity, but the prime object of the wig was to keep his head warm. When he entered his cottage by the pier, off, together, would come cap and wig as a unit, to be laid carefully on the hall table. "Come in, then," he would say to me and I would follow him, his head as bald as an egg above his lean, lined, weather-coloured face, into the neat sitting room overlooking the loch, for a cup of tea and one of Mrs. Macfarlane's scones.

We had other exciting times together on the loch, Macfarlane and I. Like all fishermen, I have lost some good ones in my day - not only the sailfish off Miami, but salmon and trout in Scottish lochs and rivers, a big pike in Virginia Water, and what must have been a giant mahseer when my line broke at the end of its wild, initial run

---

[1] Though, in 1980, a party of us from the West of Scotland Angling Club - a trout fishing club founded in 1834 and, at that, the second oldest fishing club in the World - caught twelve herring on handlines near the Gantocks off Dunoon.

in a 'tank'[1] near Mhow in India. But the one I would like to see, most of all, was the one that got away in Loch Striven. It happened when the three of us - Walter Berry, Macfarlane and myself in the bow - were jigging[2] for big 'coalies' not far off the pier, in about 20 fathoms.

We had several good fish in the boat - which Walter Berry's little cairn terrier was wrestling with and shouting at - when, on an up-tug well clear of the bottom, I hit something so heavy that I couldn't move it. I called out for help. Macfarlane tumbled forward and together, pulling with all our might, we very slowly began to line in against this heaving mass below. But it was too good to last, of course, and, suddenly, we were flat on our backs damning and blasting with nae fush. It could, I suppose, have been a very large cod or a big skate - but I shall never know in this world - and, even if one of the bonuses of Heaven is the gift to see all the good fish one has lost on earth, I somehow doubt whether I, personally, will be in a position to enjoy it.

Apart from the sea fishing in the loch, there was the Invervegain Burn, whose glen cut for a mile or more into the hills behind the shore. It was full of small 'brownies' and it was here, at 14, that I first learned the thrill of fishing for trout - up through the rocky, deep, pools in the woodland to the longer, shallower pools of the high, open moorland. It was at the head of one of the latter, in a small scoop of rock about the size of a wash tub, that I caught the record Invervegain trout - a golden 12-inch ten-ounce fish - working upstream, like a stalker, with a worm on very light tackle, wading in sand-shoed feet.

Making my way home, proudly, as that August evening fell, with my catch in my haversack amongst the worms and remains of my biscuits, I stopped to release a ram, whose handlebar horns had become entangled in a strand of wire. He didn't thank me but I didn't mind; it had been a marvelous day anyway.

While fishing one would occasionally disturb a heron, or spot a buzzard riding a thermal overhead, or put up a small covey of grouse. Walter Berry had told me that there were still a few birds on the hill and he would lend me a gun - and Macfarlane's son[3] - to walk them up if I wished. But I wasn't interested. Killing, birds or any wild animal has never attracted me - though this aversion, hypocritically I fear, has not yet extended to fish.

Jack and I gently enjoyed our short visit to Glenstriven. The Berry's were as kind and hospitable as ever - and nothing seemed to have changed. Macfarlane's wig was still red and firmly attached to his cap. Miss Berry photographed us with her camera on its wooden tripod. Walter Berry, happily, still managed to get around with the help of his sticks and his new cairn puppies. We were both relieved to hear that he had, at last, given up his morning cold bath and had accepted that he could, therefore, no longer insist on his guests taking one.

It was my last visit to Glenstriven before the Berry family, after the War, sold it

---

[1] The name in India for a reservoir. The tank at Mhow was old and large - more like a natural lake, tree and reed-bordered.

[2] In jigging, the lure consisted of a six-inch bar of shiny lead with a triangle of hooks on the end. It was lowered to the bottom, pulled up a few feet and then slowly yo-yo'd up and down to imitate a small fish in trouble.

[3] Prior to WW2, Macfarlane's two sons joined the 8th Battalion, Argyll & Sutherland Highlanders. They were both taken prisoner at the surrender of the 51st Highland Division at St Valery in June 1940.

to a Yorkshireman who modernised it - with electricity to replace the old oil lamps and candles, and central heating to boost the log fires of an evening. I am glad I saw the trees, once more, in their glorious autumn colouring and the bracken turning to rust on the hills of the far shore. And I am glad I was able to recount to Jack the memories of my boyhood days on the loch, the hill and the burn.

We made Brooklands in time for the Autumn Meeting on 17th October, after stopping at Strensall to pick up some kit for the Grand Tour of Europe we had decided upon.

The J4 and I were entered only for one short Mountain Circuit race and, though not placed, we managed to average 69.74 mph - our best speed ever over the circuit. On the downhill runs to the Fork Hairpin, the little engine was reaching 6,800 rpm, representing just over 110 mph. Alan Maclachlan must have breathed on it to some purpose while we were away in the North. As I climbed out of the car in the Paddock after the race, I realised that that was that. I was pleased I had done quite well over the season for a beginner, but I should now, I knew, never be anything more than that. Above all, however, I was content, as I had sat in the narrow cockpit at the start line, blipping the engine in time to Ebby's count-down, that the rapture of the race had, once more, enveloped me, albeit for the last time. It more than made up for that dreadful day at Wetherby a month previously.

As I have told, J4 was acquired, subsequently, by Ian Nickols, the motoring writer, who fitted an 'R' type engine together with other modifications, and raced the little car with increasing success in track and road events until the war obliterated motor racing for six years and Brooklands forever.

Nine days later, the Big MG was hoisted on board the Dover packet and carried, with Jack and me, across the Channel to Calais - not entirely as planned, however. We had stayed the previous night with the de Mey's in Hove, with the intention of catching the morning ferry from nearby Newhaven. But Jack had taken rather long to get himself and his doodle-sack organised - not, as world-wide evidence could prove, for the first time - and we missed the boat, in spite of a very brisk and rather bad-tempered drive in an effort to make up for lost time. As we watched the ship leave Newhaven without us, Jack spoke one word, "Dover!" So on we drove, madly, another seventy odd miles in pouring rain, to catch, by a short head, the afternoon boat. It was a wet, dismal crossing and Calais looked its worst under low, weeping clouds. However, the Churchill-Clark Grand Tour had, at least, begun.

Our first stop, of course, was Paris where we found a comfortable little hotel in l'Avenue de la Grande Armee, not far from l'Arc de Triomphe.

From here during the first two days, we high-mindedly, ascended the Eiffel Tower (but no piping at the top, for some reason); visited St. Cyr (the French 'Sandhurst' - which didn't impress us too much); the tomb of Napoleon at Les Invalides (which did), and Versailles, where I had stayed with my family one Easter Holidays in the early twenties. On the second evening we set out - with more frivolous aims - for Montmartre.

After a fine supper in a small restaurant - having first, at Jack's insistence, inspected, in detail, innumerable outside menus - we sought out the *Cafe des Glaces,* which had been recommended to us as an interesting port-of-call by some disreputable acquaintance back home. It was a pleasant enough place, with tables round the tall mirror-lined walls, which, no doubt, gave the cafe its name. In the centre was a small dance floor and, in one corner, stairs leading, evidently, to an upper room since, every now and then, one of the waitresses would escort a customer aloft.

After two or three post-prandial glasses of cognac and some light banter with the waitresses, we left and strolled thoughtfully down the street, smiling politely from time to time as young ladies murmured to us. At last I spoke, "I say, Jack, did you notice that every single one of the girls in the Cafe des Glaces was stark naked?" "Well," replied Jack, "you're not quite right. If you'd looked more carefully you'd have spotted that the head waitress was wearing a little apron."

The next day, after a short piping recital in the Bois de Boulogne which was well-received by the strollers, we drove out to Montlhery, some 20 miles south of Paris, to see what the Big MG would do. Not very much as it turned out, Jack, in the passenger seat, timing her best lap at only 75 mph even with the windscreen flat. However, the day was made notable for Jack by the presence of Jimmy Guthrie, who was at Montlhery attempting a number of motor cycle records on his powerful heavy shouldered Norton.

From Paris, both now dressed in the kilt, we wandered South, Riviera-bound, first calling at the Chateau Nanteuil in Blois, where my brother, Cuffy, had spent his 'language year' and around the grounds of which he had hurtled on his ancient motor bikes.

Then on we wandered, through Limoges and Brive in the Dordogne and over the Massif Central, staying, overnights, in small hotels and auberges. On most evenings, in some small cafe, without much persuasion, out would come Jack's pipes and sometimes, with considerably more persuasion, off would come my shoes and, accepting philosophically the inevitable splinters, I would try a Highland Fling or sword dance over crossed sticks to Jack's music.

There were always willing French hands to push back the chairs to make room for Jack's marching or my dancing, and, afterwards, to offer a varying amount of free wine or beer. Sometimes, men in their forties or more would come forward, recalling *lajupe* - the kilt - from the Great War, and then, perhaps, the wine would flow more freely and Jack and I would listen to long, half-understood tales - probably of Verdun, through which, to its cost most of the French Army had passed during 1916. Occasionally there would be a veteran with the thin red and green ribbon of the *Croix de Guerre* or plain red rosette of the *Legion d'Honneur* in his buttonhole, which might result in a special evening of piping, communal singing and dancing and entente cordiale from which Jack and I would wend our way to our beds, our heads brimming over with wine.

I have little doubt, in retrospect, that Jack and I, as wandering minstrels, could have earned, in cash or kind, more than a subaltern's pay of 10 bob a day - and for a while, anyway, we would have found it more fun than peacetime soldiering in Yorkshire. But then, how could I have got on without my No. 2 Platoon! In fact, Jack and I had worked up quite a good turn together, stemming from a piping and dancing performance we had given, the previous December, at a charity show in the ballroom of the Oatlands Park Hotel, near Weybridge, while I had been on my fencing course at the PT School.

Fortunately, on that occasion, there had been no experts from North of the Border in the audience and our act had gone down well, aided in my case by the red and white striped Loretto swimming trunks I had thoughtfully - since we performed on a high stage - worn beneath my kilt. Much of the applause, I gathered afterwards, had been attributable to these fine undergarments.

The drive itself was a pleasure. The weather was mild and dry, we seldom put up the hood and sometimes, even, lowered the windscreen, replacing it with the small aero screens, which, at least, gave us the impression of greater speed.

Jack was, as always, the ideal passenger - relaxed, never nervous, even when the Big MG and I decided to get a hurry on. In fact, not once did he drive the car throughout the whole tour, seeming happy enough to sit and observe the world as it went by, which is, I suppose, the way to travel. It is sadly true that the driver of a car misses much. Jack, moreover, always the enterprising and clever navigator, led us through some enchanting scenery, towns and villages - often reading out a snippet of history that appealed to him from the guide book we had bought in Tours and sometimes, like Auntie Janey, calling a halt at some hilltop or riverside so that I might 'take a smoke'[1] and he might exercise his lungs on the pipes.

As I have inferred earlier, Jack was very particular about his personal appearance, and it would amuse me to watch him, out of the corner of my eye, as we approached some village or town. The rear view mirror would be pulled round, he would check the angle of his bonnet, the sweep of his moustache and the set of the bright Macmillan plaid across his shoulder and then, as we passed slowly down the main street he would smile and raise his hand to les francais, most of whom would stare blankly back in surprise, though some might wave and grin at the long black car with its two members of the Auld Alliance.

Having reached (for the very first time) the Mediterranean, our general destination, we settled for a few days in an hotel in Cannes owned by a retired major of the Swiss Army and his wife, in whose parlour we would sit during the evenings to listen to the BBC. The major and his wife were already, in early November 1936, disturbed by the threat to our monarchy caused by the liaison of King Edward VIII (whom Jack and I still thought of as the Prince of Wales) with Mrs Simpson, especially since the King had for so long been a popular figure on the Riviera scene.

They seemed, moreover, to know a great deal more about the problem than we did, no doubt because the media at home were still maintaining, under Beaverbrook's persuasion, a self-imposed silence on the issue. No such restrictions, however, applied to the Continental press, which was making a distasteful meal of it. In fact, in Britain, the crisis was to surface, wholly, only a little more than a week before the actual Abdication on 11th December.

In Cannes we had hoped to find sunshine and fun. In the event we found mild, watery warmth and, except for the palm trees on the sea front, the feel of Hove in the off-season. I have a movie, taken by Jack, of myself in the white tweed coat I had bought in January at Abercrombie & Fitch in New York[2], and rolled up grey flannels—paddling in the empty Mediterranean below the promenade and, by the look on my face, not enjoying it much. The only truly bright memory remaining of Cannes is of Jack and I setting out, one evening, in the Big MG to sample and list as many different aperitives as we could find. From bar to bar we moved, Jack writing down, more and more haltingly as the evening progressed, each new discovery - of which there seemed to be an unending variety - some, simply, horrid.

Afterwards, we drove back to the hotel through the quiet, autumn, night streets of

---

[1] Jack has never smoked. If asked why, his standard answer is, "It's too difficult."

[2] I had bought this after seeing Robert Taylor wearing a white tweed coat in the film Magnificent Obsession. Vanity! Vanity!

Cannes, with Jack, squatting on the back of the car, piping with all his might while I sang loudly to the tunes I knew. No one expostulated - or perhaps we were too exh- -ilerated by the fumes of Dubonnet, Pernod Fils and St. Raphael to notice if they did.

The next morning, over some very black coffee, Jack looked at me - "Italy?", he queried. "All right", I said. "We might as well get some new stamps on our passports". So, having strapped on our kilts and packed a few essentials - leaving the bulk of our gear at the hotel - we set out eastward along the winding Corniche road, via Nice, Monte Carlo, Menton and the Italian frontier post at Bordighera, intending to be back in a couple of days.

In the event, ("What about going on till we're fed up?" - "OK. Time is, fortunately for once, not of the essence."), it was nearly six weeks before we returned to the bosom of the Hotel Helvetia in Cannes - by which time we were two possibly wiser, but certainly poorer young men.

It was somewhere between Nice and the Italian border that we found our first, self-imposed trial. Off a rocky headland, far below the road, Jack spotted a wreck - a cargo ship of about 500 tons. It lay almost upright, with decks awash, some fifty yards offshore - abandoned but, apparently, little damaged. I stopped the car and we looked at each other. Then, without a word, Jack collected his pipes from the boot and we made our way across a field to the edge of the cliff, round, with considerable difficulty, an overhanging wire fence and thence down the cliff face to the rocks opposite the wreck.

The green, streaky sea at the water's edge, under an overcast sky, looked much rougher than it had from above - but by then we were committed. And so, after stripping to the skin and some 'apres vous-ing', we leapt into the distressingly cold water and splashed out through the swell to the wreck, climbing on board amidships and thence up onto the bridge. After pottering around for a few minutes and remarking how little evident damage there was, I swam back to the shore and began to dry myself with my vest, expecting Jack to be right behind me. But I should have known better; he had found his way into the cabins below the bridge and was, obviously, totally absorbed in exploration.

Eventually, I yelled loudly and he appeared on deck, waved, then posed, full-frontal, on the midship rail for a moment before diving neatly into the surf and crawling ashore. As he climbed onto the rocks I saw around his neck a length of line, on which he had threaded a number of brass souvenirs of our visit to the wreck of a vessel whose name and port of origin I have long forgotten. To seal the event, Jack picked up his pipes and, still naked, played, with feeling, a lament for a lost, lonely ship. I didn't dance.[1]

Our drive along the coast road - with its innumerable steep hills and hairpin bends - was hard work for the driver, since it was becoming apparent that the front geometry of the big MG was not all it should be, exacerbated, no doubt, by the weight of the stupid mass of badges I had strung on heavy bars forward of the radiator. However, in Genoa, we found a small dark garage in a side street with an inspired meccanico, who, enthralled by a car he had never seen before, breathed on the front assembly with such typical Italian skill, that it remained greatly improved thereafter. So, on we went, looking into Rapallo - "lovely little place" - and Viareggio - "long,

---

[1] Many years later, Jack wrote from Cannes to ask me whether or not we should submit a claim to the GBR as the first Mediterranean super-streakers.

sandy beach, but very much a resort" - to Livorno[1], which I had to see.

In Livorno, where we stayed a couple of nights, as well as having a good look round the town and port, we somehow got involved with the lady singer who was top of the bill at the town's variety theatre - so much so that, at one moment, we found ourselves on the stage beside her, to the noisy astonishment of the audience. After the performance, we took her out to supper.

She was tall, dark and handsome, spoke French - and was rather nice. When we suggested, quite innocently, that she might care to come back to our hotel - a pretty seedy establishment, I seem to remember - for a nightcap (though we must have used some other term), she excused herself by saying that she was going to Confession early the next morning. As C of E's - by Army definition - this was the first time either Jack or I had heard that excuse used to refuse a drink. However, she came with us to Pisa the next day and, high-mindedly, we climbed the Leaning Tower - the Campanile - together and looked down on the magnificent cathedral, its Duomo white as snow in the clear Tuscan air.

From Pisa we pressed on a further 200 miles - still far from fed up - to Roma, where, to enjoy a bit of luxury, we stayed the first night at the Albergo Bristol, in the Piazza Barberini.

It was a fortunate choice, as it turned out. Very early the next morning I was woken by distant singing. Hardly had I become aware of this, when there was a bang on my door and Jack's voice calling, "Rex! Quick!" I leapt out of bed, opened the door, Jack grabbed me, still half asleep, by the arm and pulled me along to his room, whose small balcony overlooked the Piazza. The rude awakening was worth it.

Marching, with rifles at the slope, down the hill of the Via Vittorio Veneto on our right, and passing below us were endless, eight-deep columns of infantry in grey-green uniforms - Alpini, in their Tyrolean bonnets; Bersaglieri, with plumed hats, and infantry of the line in steel helmets — preceded by bands and singing, in turn, with all their might those stirring, Blackshirt marching songs - Ino a Roma, Faccetta Nera and Giovinezza.[2] It was a splendid sight and Jack and I, as professional soldiers, were intrigued and entranced - and impressed. At breakfast we learned it was the Queen's Birthday and that the troops had been marching to the Piazza Venezia where, later in the morning, a Parade was to be held in Her honour in front of the Vittorio Emanuele II Memorial. Our waiter also told us that Il Duce was going to speak from his balcony in the Palazzo Venezia, overlooking the Square, sometime during the day.

So, after breakfast, off we hastened along the Via del Quirinale to the Piazza - on the way to be given an officious rocket by one policeman for walking on the wrong pavement and another, by a second, for haphazardly crossing the street.[3] In the

---

[1] Known as Leghorn, it was, intermittently, a British naval base during the Napoleonic Wars. During this part of our tour I was, by happy chance, reading Hervey Allen's best-selling novel *Anthony Adverse* (Gollancz - 1934), in which the town plays a central part.

[2] There were also some rather dispirited-looking, dismounted heavy cavalry, with their own brass band - but the less said about them the better! Their band was no doubt playing, "Where have all the horses gone?"

[3] Pedestrians were very regimented in central Rome at that time. Pavements were "one way" and street crossing areas marked and enforced. The extent to which Mussolini managed to discipline the easy-going, individualistic Italian civilians was quite remarkable.

*Alpini troops at the Queen's Birthday parade*

*The Vittorio Emanuele II monument in the Piazza Venezia as the backdrop for the Queen's Birthday Parade - 1936*
*The corner of the Palazzo Venezia is on the right*

*Jack moving a Chianti cart so I could extract the big MG - whose De Havilland Comet (G-ACSS)mascot can just be seen at the foot of the photograph - "not a patch on our macchi" thinks the Italian on the right*

*The big MG on the Appian Way*

immense square, behind the paraded infantry, was a great crowd, which gave warm applause to their tiny King and Queen when they appeared on the steps below the vast, white memorial - while the troops cheered, like ours, on command.

After their rather pathetic, but dignified Majesties had left, the crowd, buzzing by now, edged towards the large building in the right-hand corner of the Piazza, look- ing up expectantly at the balcony which jutted out from the central second floor window.

Slowly and spasmodically at first they began to chant - "Duce! Duce!" After what seemed a long wait, a heavy-faced, heavy-shouldered torso in grey uniform, topped by a tasselled black cap - rather like a rounded fez - appeared on the balcony.

The chant grew staccato and fortissimo; the figure raised its arm in stiff Roman salute, slowly turning from side to side - and then it was gone. Mussolini - Il Duce - in person! He had said nothing - wisely leaving the honours of the day with the Monarchy.

Perhaps it was this ceremonial parade - or just Jack's romanticism that encouraged us to visit the marble tomb in St. Peter's at the Vatican of 'King James III', better known as Prince Charles Edward Stuart - 'Bonnie Prince Charlie' - the Young Pretender of the 1745 Rebellion and his Father 'The Old Pretender'. No pipe music - not even 'Lochaber No More' - was allowed in the great cathedral, though we both murmured a prayer for the men of Prince Charles's 'Manchester Regiment', most of whom, finally, had died on the gallows.

That night, still dressed in the kilts we had worn all day as a compliment to the Queen, Jack and I dined in a small ristorante, recommended to us by the Hall Porter at the Bristol - an excellent man. It lay up a narrow lane, bounded on one side by a high stone wall. As we entered, the proprietor came forward to welcome us - but stopped suddenly, broke into excited Italian and, to our indignation ("Hey! We're English [or Scottish] - you can't do this to us"), pushed us back to the door. However, the cause of his excitement soon became apparent, when, surrounded by waiters, cooks and his family, he pointed dramatically across the lane to a large poster on the wall. It was an advertisement for the film, "The Ghost Goes West." Robert Donat, the star, was dressed, in glorious colour, in full Highland rig-kilt, doublet, plaid and diced hose. We got a free glass of vino vecchio on that - but had to pay for our dinner.

It was later that night, back at the hotel, that we first met Dina and Marisa. They were sitting in the lounge, looking quite stunning, the one dark, the other fair - with two officers of the Blackshirt militia - whom Jack later classified as 'pretty bogus'! After staring for some while with apparent interest at our Highland garb, one of the officers came over and invited us to join them in, of all things, a minute black coffee. After some laughing chit-chat in halting Anglo-French-Italian, the girls told us they were going down to Naples in a few days time in Dina's Fiat Millecento to visit some undisclosed relation.

We then told them this was good news as we had also decided to drive on down there, with the aim of visiting the island of Capri, with which I had been enchanted since reading Axel Munthe's book, "*The Story of San Michele*"[1] - and, though to a lesser extent, by the song - "T'was on the Isle of Capree that I found her ..."!

---

[1] *The Story of San Michele* by Axel Munthe (John Murray 1929); a best seller in 25 languages. A doctor of medicine, Munthe also wrote, anonymously, a book about the terrible cholera epidemic in Naples in 1883 with which he was closely and nobly concerned. He died in the Royal Palace in Stockholm in 1942, aged 92.

A few days later found us at another Albergo Bristol - in Naples this time - about 130 miles further south - but not before, high-mindedness to the fore, we had 'done' Rome and the villages around it, including Tivoli, Frascati and Monte Rotundo with guide book, note book and camera. Jack on these occasions was a great companion. Obscure and minor historical happenings provided him with the breath of life and, moreover, he had the happy knack of communicating such events in vivid style to those, such as myself, with similar enthusiasms.

The drive to Napoli included a short diversion onto the Appian Way - for the record - and a very fast run on a long, straight stretch of road beside a canal, along which, on the return journey, the Big MG was to maintain 90 mph indicated for nearly 15 miles. But we were in a real hurry by that time.

In Naples we found we were once more in the thick of things. The day after we arrived a Naval Review was being held for the benefit of Admiral Horthy, the Hungarian dictator.

Jack and I, kilted again, walked the short distance to the Via Marittima - the harbour-side road - from which, over the heads of the spectators and troops lining the route, we could see an impressive forest of naval masts of all shapes and sizes, with Vesuvius, lazily smoking, as a far distant backdrop.

We were not, however, impressed by the platoon of Alpini behind which we were standing. The crowd was fraternising with the men, passing them lit cigarettes to pull at and baiting the young officer, a 'tenente', who, with drawn sword, was, in theory, but not in fact, in command. We felt sorry for the poor lad, who would come bustling between the ranks to scold his men, only to be met with
laughs and jeers from the populace. Further annoyance was to follow, when, after a long delay in the arrival of Il Duce and the Admiral, Jack and I felt the need to relieve nature and walked over to an open pissoir in the corner of the piazza behind us. We hadn't, however, allowed for the curiosity of the Neapolitans, who followed to find out, at first hand, the answer to that oldest of questions facing Scotsmen wearing the kilt. So back we went, instead, to the hotel, returning just in time to see the two 'great men', escorted by a squadron of 'household cavalry', passing in a long, open car - a special Fiat or Lancia? - and looking pretty serious about it.

We had, by now, definitely decided to spend a few days in Capri, which stood out, in splendid profile - like 'Bali Hai' - 20 miles away at the far apex of that Bay in which, it crossed my mind Nelson's great ships of the line had lain in immaculate, disciplined array both before and after the Battle of the Nile in 1798.

However, a couple of days after the Review we had managed to track down Dina and Marisa - minus Blackshirt officers - to the former's aunt's house in Posilipo, a western suburb of Naples astride the shore road. They were a rare couple - Dina, the older, dark; Marisa, fair - a perfect complement in looks and temperament to each other. One or the other of them, at any given moment, was either talking, laughing, gesticulating, singing or making a scene. By and large, we understood what they said or meant - and guessed the rest. They were marvelous company - in small doses. As for 'Auntie' - plump and smooth-faced - she was, I felt, torn between admiration for the sleek, black car and horror at the barbarous appearance of the escorts her niece and her friend had chosen. But she got used to us, and, in time, we even made her laugh.

With the two girls as company, we explored the rough and the smooth of Naples - sometimes, hair-raisingly, in the Fiat with Dina, an embodied Fury, at the wheel. On

23

one day, we made our windswept way, in the Big MG, with the screen down, along the new autostrada to Vesuvius. In 1936 - and maybe, still - one could drive up a lumpy, lava road to a small car park below the summit, whence one had to make one's way for some distance, on foot, to the huge lava-floored crater. Here we found a scattering of seedy-looking, unofficial guides, over-anxious in the off-season to conduct the scozzesi and their Roman signorine. However, Dina spat non-stop fire at them for about 15 seconds, and they retired, grinning sheepishly, though the girls, subsequently, each deigned to accept from them a small gift in the shape of a lava ash-tray.

Jack, meanwhile, doodle-sack under arm, had a more ambitious objective in mind; he was determined to climb the central cone of ash — the 'boiler house chimney' of the volcano. No guide would go with us, however, until, finally, we discovered a boy asleep on a warm slab of lava, who on being awakened by Dina and Marisa (he must have thought he had died in his sleep and arisen in some angelic heaven) and being shown a handful of lire, volunteered to take us up. So, leaving the girls behind, we scrambled up the steep side of the cone, the hard, jagged lumps of ash sliding away beneath our feet, the crepe rubber soles of my shoes melting beneath me, until we stood on the lip itself, looking down on the swirling, bottomless pit of smoke and steam.

At intervals, there would be a quiet rumble and hiss, and suddenly, out of the steam, an accumulation of stones and debris would shoot straight up to 50 feet or more before dropping back into the pit.

When this happened, the boy and I would cower back, hunching our head and shoulders protectively. To me, it felt eerie, primeval - beyond man's control. To Jack, however, it was glorious drama. He stood there, his Macmillan kilt bright against the grey smoke, chin up, fingers working, left elbow rhythmically squeezing the sack, right foot tapping the beat - playing a wild, heathen dance to Vulcan, the Roman fire-god.

The girls, on the floor of the crater below, were, meanwhile, with Roman arrogance, happily keeping the guides and a number of other characters who had, presumably, arisen from their lava couches, strictly in their lowly Neapolitan places.

Having finished with Vesuvius, we drove over to Pompeii, where there was much thumbing of the guide book by Jack and some wild, immodest laughter from the girls at the mild erotica in one section of the quite remarkable ruins of this one-time Roman 'Brighton'. At dusk, all weary, we repaired to the large hotel nearby - at this time of year virtually empty - for a large meal of assorted pasta and lacrima cristi wine from the vineyard on the slopes of the volcano. At midnight we left, aiming for the lights of Naples. It was a bright, starry night - but very cold. The Big MG and I cruised slowly and quietly along the empty autostrada. Marisa, beside me, was nestled, asleep, in the teddy bear rug. Behind us, Jack and Dina, in the dickey, sat cocooned together in Jack's plaid, the tops of their heads - ebony and silver - just visible.

It had been a good outing.

On the day the girls left Napoli to return to Roma, we gave them a noonday meal at a tiny ristorante above Posilipo, looking out across the shining water to Capri and the Sorrento peninsular. The Fiat had arrived - Dina, eyes flashing, at the wheel - in a stylish skid, with Marisa, beside her, apparently unmoved at the prospect of a 130

*Vesuvius crater with the cone in the centre*

*The Heavy cruiser 'Pola' of the 10,000 ton Zara Class*

mile, death-defying drive that afternoon. At any rate, they both ate their pasta like good girls, but not before there had been something of a scene over the vino.

We had ordered a bottle of Capri rosso, but, on its arrival we noticed it had no label and the girls, indignant, argued with the proprietor as to its origin - to me surprisingly like the first one, so I handed it, for a second opinion, to Marisa who, after a quick inspection, really went to town on the waiter - speaking incredibly rapidly, yet enunciating every word perfectly, at one moment with her little chest pushed out and her face pink with fury and at the next slumped down in despair, almost, but not quite, at a loss for words.

It was a magnificent performance and, when she finally stopped, exhausted, Jack's and my applause was echoed by laughter and bravos, not only from the waiter, but from southern Italian faces which had appeared from nowhere to peep through windows and round doors. As for the wine, we drank it because it was, I suspect, the only bottle they had. It was a very small ristorante and times were hard in Napoli.

The following day, having parked the car in the hotel garage, Jack and I embarked in the vaporetto for Capri. As we steamed out of Naples harbour I photographed some of the fine ships of the Italian Navy which had assembled for Admiral Horthy's Review, including the 'Pola' and three other 10,000 ton, 8-inch gun cruisers of the 'Zara' and 'Trento' classes, and a host of destroyers. Jack and I, ship-lovers both, were impressed not only by their smartness but by their stylish lines - which the Italian genius seems always able to impart even to inanimate objects.

During the 90-minute voyage Jack gave a short piping recital which was received with a mixture of interest and levity by both passengers and crew. Fortunately, the movement of the ship - and, of course, the danger of splinters from the wooden deck - made dancing impracticable.

We had intended to stay in Capri for only a few days, but, quickly overtaken by the island's spell, in the event stayed three weeks. The first night we spent at the Quisisana Hotel - luxurious and expensive. The next morning, however, while sipping Americanos in the sunny piazza - the social centre of the island - we were fortunate enough to meet Leslie Lang the painter[1] who, like a number of other escapists - had become resident in Capri. On his advice we moved into rooms in a small friendly albergo, more suited to our falling finances, in one of the narrow streets off the piazza. From then on, for my part, I was happy enough to allow the languorous air of this idyllic island embrace me without further resistance. But Jack, unfortunately, was made of sterner stuff and certain tasks had first to be accomplished. Of these, some were planned - some just happened.

But first, I had better briefly describe this beautiful island - Isola di Capri - for the benefit of those readers who have not yet had the good fortune to visit it for themselves.

Capri is about 3/4 miles long from East to West and about 1 3/4 miles at its widest point. The island consists of two plateaus - the western one the higher - separated, in the middle, by cliffs and a saddle of lower ground. The main harbour, Marina Grande, is at the centre of the Naples side of the island; the Marina Piccola (the little harbour) is on the opposite side of the 'waist' facing south. The town of Capri lies about four

---

[1] Leslie William Lang RBA - born 1886: Studied at the Slade School of Art and in Italy. Exhibited at Royal Academy (1909 - Umbria - Cat. No 916) Royal Society of British Artists, the provinces and abroad.

hundred feet above the main harbour, from which it was reached by funicular railway - funiculare - in a few minutes, or up a steep, winding road on foot or in a horse-drawn carrozza. ( There were no taxis or private cars in Capri in 1936). The eastern plateau was covered by a network of mule tracks and footpaths leading from the town to villas, 'crofts' and historical remains, including - on the abrupt cliffs at the far end - the ruins of the Palazzo di Tiberio, looking across to the Sorrento peninsular.

The highest point on the eastern plateau is Monte Tuoro at 869 feet. The western and wilder - plateau, reached from Capri town by a steep road that winds up the cliffs which divide the island (or by the 777 Phoenician steps if you are feeling energetic), is topped by Monte Solaro, at 1,932 feet, the summit of Capri. Below Solaro, to the north, lies the scattered village of Anacapri, with its olive and pine trees and walled mule-tracks. At the north-eastern end of the village, on the very edge of the cliffs, stands Axel Munthe's fabulous Villa San Michele with its sublime view across the Bay of Naples, which I was so anxious to visit. Axel Munthe himself, however, almost blind by that time, had retreated to the isolated Torre Materita - formerly part fortress, part monastery - reached by a mile-long mule track winding through olive groves south-westward from the village centre.

Virtually the whole of Capri, except for the small harbour area, is girt by cliffs, most of them dropping sheer into blue water and cut into by numerous coves and grottos - including the world-famous Blue Grotto at the north-western corner. At the south-east corner of the island, to complete the picture, the astonishing Faraglioni rocks rise over 300 feet straight out of the sea.

The 'tasks' that Jack had laid down for us to accomplish were, in the event, good fun and not too arduous. We climbed the long stony track to Monte Solaro on a beautiful clear day, having first taken a carrozza up to Anacapri - the cocchiere, traditionally, singing 'O Sole Mio' on the way, breaking off long enough to doff his cap as we passed the shrine to the Madonna della Grotta on the cliff-side below the ruined *Castello di Barbarossa,* named after the legendary sea-raider.

From the summit we looked down, with delight, across the town of Capri to Tiberius's Palace on the far cliffs and, beyond, over the royal blue water to Sorrento on the mainland. On the return to Anacapri, we made straight for the Villa San Michele, which for me, as I have told, epitomized Capri.

In the event, however, I came away with a feeling of disappointment - not with the building, or its pillars, its stained glass windows and mosaics or its classical antiquities - and certainly not with its stunning view across the Bay of Naples from its position on the very edge of the cliffs - but with the Sphinx. The Sphinx, which Munthe, while building his villa, had dreamed was lying in a remote cave on the mainland, and which he had found, exactly as in his dream, and had brought back in his sailing cutter to San Michele.

The huge, smooth granite sphinx was there all right - "crouching on the parapet of the chapel . . . with its stony, wide open eyes" - but, when I waxed lyrical over the mystical story of its discovery, the old signora who had guided us round and who spoke excellent English, looked at the young man before her and said gently, "Signor, you must learn not to believe everything you read."

Monte Tuoro had, of course, also to be climbed as the complement of Solaro, but this involved little more than an hour from our table in the Piazza. More exciting was our circuit of the Faraglioni in kayaks - and leaky ones at that. It came about through our growing habit of spending the days down at the 'bathing station' at the Marina

The Faraglioni Rocks
Jack - 1936

Jack -1968
Thirty two years further on
(Photograph by Rosamund Churchill)

*I won 2nd prize for this picture at a 'photographic salon ' in Ismailia
(Jack is absorbed in a week-old 'Times')
(Photographed in Egypt in 1937. The Suez press captioned it
'Ecossais au bord de l'eau')*

Piccola, where we would swim in the cool clear sea, sunbathe on the tiny beach or on the rocks flanking it, and - looking across to the Faraglioni a mile or so away - eat spaghetti and drink Capri rosso or bianco in the little restaurant - which was to become associated increasingly over the years with the name of Gracie Fields and her Caprese husband, Boris.

Eventually - and inevitably - Jack decided we must paddle round the Faraglioni in a couple of the kayaks one could hire at the beach. So, after lunch one day, stripped to the waist and fortified by vino - no life jackets in those days and no idea what to do if we capsized - we set out over the gentle southerly swell on the two-mile paddle round the giant rocks. As, finally, we passed, side by side, into the cold dark between them, the swell increased alarmingly and, from the cliffs on either side, echoed, dramatically, the crash of breakers. We were glad when we broke out again into the warm sunlight and smoother water.

Another but less successful outing, was conceived one day by Jack as we sat with Leslie Lang, sipping pre-lunch aperatives, at our accustomed table in the Piazza. Leslie and I were chatting about the portraits of Jack and myself that he was painting at the time, while Edouardo, the young waiter who had adopted the two scozzesi, leant protectively against the wall of the trattoria behind us. Jack, meanwhile, was looking through a short history of Capri, given him by Leslie.

Suddenly, Jack turned to me, the book in his lap. "Rex!" he exclaimed. "It says here that when the French captured Capri from the British in 1808 by a sea-borne assault up the cliffs at Orico, at the far end of the island, the British garrison - mostly Maltese and Corsicans - escaped to the Marina Grande, where the Royal Navy embarked them, by climbing down that cliff." He swung round and pointed to the Anacapri cliffs that divide the island. "What's more, it adds" - and he looked down at the book - "that only one poor fellow fell and lost his life." "Oh, God!" I thought. "It can't be!" But it could - and that very afternoon, fortified once more (with Chianti this time) and clad, still in kilts and walking shoes, we marched from the Piazza, through the pines and olives and small vineyards covering the waist of the island, to the foot of the sheer Anacapri cliffs. Here, Jack, after looking up at the vertical face, eyes alight with anticipation, declared, "Well, they always say it's easier to climb up than down - let's go" - or its anglicised equivalent.

Raising my eyes, sourly, from my shoes, past which eroded debris from the cliff face was slowly sliding, I must have muttered, "Dopo voi, Jackie", because without wasting further words, he began to climb - and I followed. About 20 minutes later we stopped, glued to the cliff-face about 50 feet up, Jack's feet at the level of my eyes. I called out, "How's it going?" Jack called back, "I'm stuck." "So am I", I replied. "Let's go back." After a long, stubborn pause, he said, "I can't," to which I added, "Neither can I." He was right; it *is* easier to climb up than down. We did, eventually, with scraped knees and elbows, get back to what was, to me, happily, terra firma, but to Jack, simply a defeat - not to be referred to again - nor softened, either, by the excuse that neither of us had previously climbed anything more demanding than a rope and wall bars in a gymnasium.

We discovered later that the garrison had, in fact, descended the 777 Phoenician steps and not the cliff; that the 'one poor fellow' had, so to speak, fallen downstairs. Thus our honour was, to some extent, satisfied.

It was not long after what we came to call 'the recce', that Jack and I decided it was high time we left for home. The decision was due, not only to our critical shortage of funds, but also to our increasing worry about the situation at home, which now, at the beginning of December 1936, was being given leading publicity in the continental edition of the *Daily Mail* and in *The Times,* which Leslie Lang received by post. Somehow, Jack and I felt we should be in Britain at this time of danger to the Monarchy, in case 'all good men and true' - as Jack and I conceitedly, considered ourselves to be - were needed. We spent many hours discussing the crisis with Leslie Lang and other expatriate residents, including Teddy Gerard, a delightful, retired actress, who enchanted us with racy stories of her past - and with other memories of her friends and enemies.

On the whole, Jack and I were of the opinion that Edward VIII - our *Prince of Wales* -should stay on the throne, but we were split as to whether he should break off his liaison with Mrs Simpson or marry her - morganatically if necessary. I tended to prefer the former, while Jack favoured the latter course. In fact, it was over this issue that Jack and I - for the first and last time - came near to blows while walking home late one night. In the narrow, empty street we squared up to each other, fists clenched, breathing fire and vino - and then, suddenly, foolishly, burst out laughing at the absurdity of it and swung back to our albergo, arm in arm, in step to a hummed "Nut Brown Maiden."

I have, incidentally, over the years, been asked how Jack and I - both 'loners' to some extent - put up with each other's company, without friction, for so long. I can only say, again, that we have always accepted each other's attitudes to life, without criticism. In writing of Jack, I have, perhaps, tended to parody his objectivity, whereas, in truth, his saving grace - which has I hope come through - is that he has never allowed his determination to outpace his sense of humour.

We left Capri on 9th December 1936. At a farewell party in the Piazza at mezzogiorno on the day before, Leslie Lang, for whom we had both been sitting over the previous fortnight, produced our portraits, placing them, with the help of Edouardo, on tables against the trattoria wall. There was applause - especially for the fine painting of Jack, the piper - a toast to the artist, and arrivadercis to us both. That evening, Leslie Lang presented us with black and white photographs of the portraits, which he had taken and developed himself. He also asked whether we wished to buy the portraits - painted, incidentally, in his own style of dry water colours - gouache - giving the superficial effects of oils. "How much, Leslie?" we asked. "250 guineas," he replied. "Each?", I gasped. "I'm afraid so," said Leslie. We never saw our portraits again, though they were both exhibited in 1938 at an exhibition of Leslie's work in a Bond Street gallery.

We caught the morning boat to Napoli after young Edouardo, with some emotion, had said goodbye to us at the upper funicular station. He was going to miss his scozzesi, whose patronage of his table in the Piazza had, he imagined, given him a certain standing in the eyes of his fellow camerieri.

After collecting the dusty MG - which must have wondered what we'd been up to for the past three weeks - and spending the night at an inexpensive, back street alberge, we set out, early, to drive, like the wind, the 1,500 miles to England. In Rome, we paused only long enough to allow Dina and Marisa to provide us with a pasta lunch. In Cannes we stopped the nights of the 11th and 12th at the Hotel - Helvetia - on the evening of Friday the 11th, with the Swiss major and his wife, listening miserably, unashamed tears in all our eyes, to the Abdication speech of Edward VIII - to Jack and I, our King, right or wrong. (Quite unaware that Mrs

Simpson was also listening to the speech in Cannes).

The evening of the 14th saw us in Calais - very weary. At Dover, after a filthy crossing during which I felt very ill - though Jack was unaffected - the big MG was lifted off the ship - again in pouring rain. It was the middle of the night when we reached London, Jack asleep beside me. There was no traffic about as I stopped the car, momentarily, at a crossing - but the policeman on the pavement walked slowly towards us with his hand held up. "Pardon me, sir", he asked politely, "but are you aware that you are driving on the wrong side of the road?" England felt just the same, thank God - and with a brand new King and splendid Queen to inspire us, too.

# JACK CHURCHILL
## 'UNLIMITED BOLDNESS'

### R.KING-CLARK

Lieutenant Colonel J M T Churchill DSO* MC
(1906-96)

"There is a pleasure sure in being mad,
which non but madmen know"
*Dryden*

# CONTENTS

## Part I - Page 35

Burma, The BEF, Norway, Italy, Yugoslavia, Sachsenhausen, Niederdorf, and India

## Part II - Page 46

Warminster, Palestine, Australia, and England

## Appendix - Page 53

Extracts from the Palestine Post

# DEDICATION

This book is for ROSAMUND CHURCHILL
Jack's wife for fifty-five years 1941-1998

Rosamund is the daughter of the late Sir Maurice Denny Bt Chairman of Denny's of Dumbarton, the famous Clyde shipbuilders, whose yard lay under the shadow of Dumbarton Rock and whence over the years 1844 to 1963 were launched, not only many well-known and well-fought HM warships, but a host of vessels of diverse types.

Jack and Rosamund first met when Jack was training as a Commando in the Clyde area in 1940 following Dunkirk. 1 first met them together at the Old Dumbuck Inn in the autumn of that year on returning from combined operations training (with the 2nd Division) on Loch Fyne near lnverary.

They were married in St Augustine's Church in Dumbarton in March 1941. Rosamund and Jack were a much-loved and admired couple. Moreover, Rosamund knew not only when to tighten the reins on Jack's wilder enthusiasms but equally when there was no altemative but to let him have his head - and gallop beside him. A great girl.

RKC
1 July 1997

# PART ONE

Jack Churchill was my friend and, often my companion, for over sixty years. That he was intelligent, realistic, knowledgeable on a wide range of subjects - some distinctly esoteric - none will deny; that he was by nature an individualist, a romantic, an eccentric of startling style and initiative and, above all, in war, a formidable fighting man, is equally undeniable.

The Press in World War II, realising that the exploitation of these latter qualities, coupled with his flair for 'unlimited boldness', would prove more newsworthy than the former, christened him 'Mad Jack' - and the title stuck!

\* \* \*

Jack's attitude to, and performance in, World War II was, in fact, simply an extension of the zest for living he had shown in the years prior to 1939, with the advantage of more opportunities for adventure on offer.

To appreciate more fully his wartime record it will, perhaps, help if I recount a little of his background and some of his more unique activities during those pre-war years.

John Malcolm Thorpe Fleming Churchill, a member of an Oxfordshire family with a distinguished pedigree, was born in 1906, the eldest of three sons of Alec and Elinor Churchill. His father was for many years Director of Public Works, Hong Kong. After the Dragon School, Oxford, and King William's College, Isle of Man, followed by Sandhurst, Jack was commissioned into the Manchester Regiment on 4th February 1926. He served with its 2nd Battalion in Burma and India between 1926 and 1932, including service in the 1930-32 Rebellion in Burma, for which he received the Indian General Service Medal with Burma clasp - his first ribbon.[1]

He was at that time - and continued to be throughout his lifetime - a keen motor-cyclist. In April 1927, at the end of a Signals Course in Poona, to which he had been sent from Rangoon and whither he had taken, as company, his 1923 OHV Zenith bike, he decided to ride the 1500 miles across India to catch the boat at Calcutta to return to his Battalion. The ride, almost certainly never attempted before on a motor-cycle, came to a halt near Indore, in Central India, when he ran into a water buffalo, which had bolted across his bows bringing his journey to a temporary halt - though he later completed the journey.

In Burma, in 1926, also on the Zenith, he had driven down the railway line - there was no road from Maymyo, via Mandalay to Rangoon - some five hundred miles to visit 'a friend'. It was the bridges over the numerous kyaungs (river beds) that were the problem," Jack once told me. "There was nothing between the sleepers so I had to steer the bike by hand along a rail, while I stepped from sleeper to sleeper." But he made it!"

While staying with the Cameron Highlanders at Maymyo Jack was enchanted by the Regiment's pipe band and became a pupil of their fine pipe major. Later, back in England, he was tutored by Donald Fraser, an ex-pipe major of the Seaforths, who had

---

[1] His younger brother, Tom, followed Jack into the Manchesters and served with him in Burma, and, in 1944, in the Adriatic, as his brigade commander. Tom retired in 1962 as Major General T.B.L. Churchill, CB CBE MC. Jack's younger brother, Buster, was killed in action off Malta while serving as a pilot with the Fleet Air Arm.

piped at the battle of Tel-el-Kebir in Egypt in 1882. In due course Jack became an outstanding performer on the great highland war pipe.

In 1932, Jack was posted home, rejoining, in 1934, the 2nd Manchesters at Strensall, near York, at the conclusion of the Battalion's fourteen-year foreign tour - in Burma, India, the Andaman Islands, the Sudan and Cyprus. It was in the Manchesters at Strensall in that year, via my Scottish school (Loretto) and Sandhurst that I first met Jack and we became firm friends in the subaltern style.

Two years later, in 1936, after ten years service, Jack, aged twenty-nine, resigned his commission. It would not be unfair to say that his attitude to soldiering at that time was, as Dryden puts it:

*"Pleased with the danger, when the waves went high,*
*He sought the storms but for a calm unfit..."*

Perhaps certain eccentricities - brought on no doubt through frustration - such as piping the orderly officer to the Guard Room at three o'clock of a morning and studying the wrong pre-set Campaign in preparation for his promotion exam, precluded any chance of promotion for the time being and made the break, after a chat with his commanding officer, inevitable

In August 1936 I was involved in an aeroplane accident. After the hospital had released me, the Army sent me off on several months' sick leave. At a loss as to what to do with so much free time, I asked Jack to join me in a thrash through Europe in my car. Jack jumped at the idea and from October 1936 to January 1937 we managed to get involved (as recounted in *Free for a Blast*) in a series of escapades - some hilarious, some, to me, alarming in the extreme - all at Jack's instigation - and all helped by our kilts and the pipes! It was this expedition that first brought home to me the stuff that Jack was really made of.

For the next two years - which I spent with our overseas battalion, the 1st Manchesters - Jack, back home, involved himself in a not-altogether successful commercial venture touching on the Spanish Civil War; continued to pipe so successfully that he was placed second in the Officers Class of the Piping Championships held during the Aldershot Tattoo in June 1938 - the only Englishman out of some seventy entrants (the Daily Mirror headline read 'Englishman beats many Scots pipers' - a kind of 'man bites dog' item), and developed his skill at archery (which he had taken up as a hobby while at the Regimental Depot on his return from Burma) to the extent that he was selected as a member of the British team for the World Archery Championships in Oslo in 1939. He got back to England from this event only just in time to follow his true vocation, War.

During the Phoney War - September 1939 to 10th May 1940 - Jack and I both served in the BEF with the 2nd Manchesters - the 1st Corps machine gun battalion placed under command of the 2nd Division - digging defences we were never to use along the Belgian frontier with France. We would visit each other regularly at our respective company HQs, drink black velvet (stout and champagne at about 25p a bottle) and talk over old times and times to come. Occasionally we would make a foray into the night life of Lille, which, during those strange, eerie months, was pretty hectic.

In December 1939, Jack went off with D Company, of which he was second-in-command, for a tour of duty alongside the French Army in the Maginot Line. His patrol activity against the German outposts with his bow and war arrows during that bitterly cold winter is part of toxophilite history. Following this, he disappeared for a while, as a volunteer, into the force raised to assist the Finns against the Russian invasion of their country. This gave him a pleasant couple of weeks ski-training in Chamonix and a trip home before the expedition was cancelled.

He was back with the Manchesters for the German invasion of Holland and Belgium on 10th May 1940 - and it was at this point that Jack, as in Charles Douglas-Home's description of Rommel[1] truly became 'a man possessed, sustained almost to addiction by the adrenalin of war'. His subsequent wartime career was, in truth, quite astonishing.

Essentially an individualist, Jack, during dangerous ploys, preferred to have with him only his chosen few - 'half-backs' to his own position as 'striker' - whom he knew would react as he did. He believed, with reason that, in attack, a very small bold force, with the benefit of bluff, could often achieve greater penetration than a much larger but more lethargic body. However, he did not always keep in mind, in his enthusiasm, that the larger body would be needed, eventually, to complete the business and hold the ground gained. Or, if he did appreciate this, as commander he was rarely in a position to arrange it since, more likely than not, Jack, sword literally in hand (he had made it a personal rule always to wear his sword into battle), would be leading the attack with his 'halfbacks' at his shoulder and no one else in sight.

In defence, one cannot say more than that, if a position became untenable, he was the last to leave it - and never without a Parthian shot.

For me, as a chronicler, Jack's active war has five highlight episodes - a mix of the serious and light-hearted.

\* \* \*

The first was his performance in the latter half of May 1940 during the retreat to Dunkirk from the BEF's positions on the River Dyle, east of Brussels. Early in the three-week campaign, Tommy Woolsey (later Lieutenant Colonel E.F. Woolsey DSO), his company commander, was wounded and Jack took over command of D Company.

His outstanding achievement during the retreat, for which he was awarded the Military Cross, occurred on 27th May 1940. On that day, commanding a small, mixed force of Manchesters and other units of 4th Infantry Brigade, he held the village of l'Epinette, near Bethune, against a strong enemy attack. But what gave the action a particular Jack Churchill touch was the use of his longbow. As Donald Featherstone described it in his book *The Bowmen of England*: "Climbing into the loft of a small granary (in l'Epinette)... Captain Churchill saw, some thirty yards away, five Germans sheltering behind the wall but in clear view of the granary ... Captain Churchill lifted his bow, took careful aim and loosed the shaft to see his arrow strike the centre German in the left side of his chest and penetrate his body." Later the War Diary of HQ 4th Infantry Brigade, dated 30th May 1940, recorded: "One of the most reassuring sights of the embarkation was the sight of Captain Churchill passing down the (Dunkirk) beach with his bows and arrows. His high example and his great work.... were a great help to the 4th Infantry Brigade."

Soon after the action at l'Epinette (the news of which had not yet reached me) I

---

[1] *Rommel* by Charles Douglas-Home (Weidenfeld & Nicolson, 1973)

was sitting, chatting to a gunner officer, outside a small roadside estaminet with the remnants of my company around me, when a small moto-bicyclette came puttering towards us along the road running through the flat, deserted, Flanders fields.

    It was still some distance away when I recognised, in the sunlight of that spring of glorious weather, the pale hair and fierce moustache of the rider. I ran onto the dusty road waving my arms. The bike stopped just short of me. "Jack!" I shouted. He grinned back, the creases in his face accentuated by grime. "Ah! Hullo Clark! Got anything to drink?" - and he pulled the bike up onto its stand and joined us at the table, his strong hands, dark with dust, relaxing into his lap.

    I looked over to the bike. His longbow was tied along the frame; in one rear-wheel pannier I could see the rim of his steel helmet; from the other protruded the shafts and feathered flights of several arrows. Over the headlamp hung a German Officer's cap - a relic, Jack told us, of his action at l'Epinette. While he was talking, I noticed there was dried blood on the lobe of his left ear and on his neck. "What's that?" I asked - and he recounted how, earlier that day, when an enemy machine-gun had begun to fire bursts down a village street he was walking across, his men, behind a wall on the far side, had yelled at him run. "But I couldn't", he said, "I was too tired" - and a bullet had nicked his ear.

    It was at about the end of June 1940 - a few weeks after the Dunkirk evacuation - which, by courtesy of the Royal Navy, included, among many others, both Jack and myself - that volunteers for what became the Commandos were called for throughout the Army in Britain. The response was immediate. Jack was probably the first volunteer; this was just his cup of tea.

* * *

    The second episode - with comic opera overtones - was the part he played in his first Commando operation - the raid on Vaagso (a group of small inshore islands at the mouth of the great Nord Fjord on the West coast of Norway at latitude 62° N - some 250 miles NE of the Shetlands) on 27th December 1941, where he led in the two troops of No.3 Commando in the assault on the heavily defended coast battery on Maaloy Island. Having played his landing craft into shore to the tune of "The March of the Cameron Men" on his pipes (much to the subsequent delight of the Press), he leapt ashore, sword in hand, and disappeared into the smoke-screen already laid by Hampdens of the Royal Air Force. Fortunately, surprise was complete and the island was captured without difficulty. While celebrating the success from a case of Moselle found in the German commanding officer's hut, a demolition charge exploded nearby. The bottle broke in his hand and a piece of glass gashed his forehead deeply. The public at home were pleased with the result of the raid and Jack came in for considerable personal publicity to which he was not averse. His 'wound' healed quickly - too quickly, in fact. "I had to touch it up from time to time with Rosamund's - his wife's - lipstick to keep the wounded hero story going," he told me later.

* * *

    The third episode covers a very different occasion - and one that is already well documented. It concerns Jack's achievement, in September 1943, during the Salerno landing, the main Anglo-American assault upon Italy. At the time he was in command of No.2 Commando. On the night of 15th September Jack was ordered by the commander of 167 Infantry Brigade, under whose command he had come that day, to make a raid, with the aim of taking prisoners, up the valley towards Pigoletti, a village, strongly held by the Germans, situated on a ridge at the head of a steep, thickly wooded valley.

Jack, sword in hand, with his 'half-back', Corporal Ruffell, following 20 yards behind, outstripped the rest of his men and, in the darkness, entered the village unnoticed by the enemy.

He wrote to me later: "After capturing the first double sentry post, I handed one of the sentries over to Ruffell, put the slip knot of my revolver lanyard round the other one's neck and, with the point of my sword in his back, went and rounded up the remaining sentries - the Hun identifying himself each time when challenged - captured Pigoletti and the entire garrison of forty-two plus a 81 mm mortar and crew." Leaving the remains of one of his Troops in Pigoletti under Joe Nichol, the only surviving officer (later the Chaplain of Stowe School), Jack, with two commando soldiers, then marched the forty odd prisoners back down the steep hill to the Brigade area.

*The evening of 15th September 1943 on the Salerno beachhead - shortly before No.2 Commando's attack up the hill to Pigoletti. Jack is nearest the Camera (N.B. the hilt of his claymore above his haversack). Lieutenant-General Dick McCreery, Commander, 10th Corps, is seen pointing out the objectives with Brigadier Firth, Commander 167 Brigade of 56 (London) Division on his left and Lieutenant Colonel Cleghorne, commanding 9th Royal Fusiliers, on the far left, drinking a mug of tea.*

Later he told me, "I always bring my prisoners back with their weapons; it weighs them down. I just took their rifle bolts out and put them in a sack, which one of the prisoners carried. The prisoners also carried the mortar and all the bombs they could carry and also pulled a farm cart with five wounded in it. When we got back, I fed them with our men as if they were another troop and then sent them, along with the prisoners the other troops had captured - about a hundred in all - to the rudimentary POW cage which was virtually empty. The splendid Huns settled down to sleep after setting up their mortar with the bombs around it and carefully piling their rifles. I was told afterwards that, the next morning, they got down keenly to cleaning the mortar and their rifles after the night's dew. When the elderly dug-out who ran the (empty) POW cage appeared after breakfast he was riveted to find it fairly full. 'What was going on?' he complained to McCreary who roared with laughter."

Jack continued: "I maintain that, as long as you tell a German loudly and clearly what to do, if you are senior to him he will cry 'jawohl' and get on with it enthusiastically and efficiently whatever the surrounding situation. That is why they make such marvellous soldiers!"(What Evelyn Waugh, I seem to remember, called 'The negative joy of obedience'!)

Jack, having sent the prisoners to the cage, returned at about 1.0 am - with no rest - to the steep ridge at Pigoletti, where, over the next few days, there was "much tough fighting and counter attack, and we had quite a lot killed including the Duke of Wellington, who was in my Commando." In fact, Hilary St. George Saunders relates in his book *The Green Beret*,[1] that 2 Commando and 41 Royal Marine Commando suffered 'three hundred and sixty-seven killed, wounded or missing out of the seven hundred and thirty-eight officers and men who fought at Salerno between 9th and 19th September 1943 - almost half their strength.' We lost no prisoners.

I have always understood that Jack was recommended for the Victoria Cross *(see page 57)* for his outstanding performances at Pigoletti on the 15th September - which it has been said, saved the Salerno beachhead at a critical time. Somewhere along the line - perhaps because of the individualistic nature of his achievement (Jack himself described it as 'a bit Errol Flynn-ish'!) - it was diluted to a DSO. Whether this is true or not, VCs have certainly been awarded for lesser deeds of valour.

\* \* \*

The fourth episode spans the period from June 1944 to April 1945. On the night of 3/4th June 1944, Jack was taken prisoner during the assault on the Island of Brac[2] on the Dalmatian Coast, launched from the nearby island of Vis. This latter island was the 2nd Special Service Brigade's base in the Adriatic, from which, together with Yugoslav partisan forces, it was harassing and tying down German formations on the coast. Jack's part in this operation is described in detail in Hilary St. George Saunders' book. It tells how Jack, in command of the assault force and in company with a very large Yugoslav partisan unit[3] led the night attack on Hill 622, the key feature, playing his pipes at the head of 40 Royal Marine Commando (commanded by Lieutenant

---

[1] Published by Michael Joseph in 1949.

[2] Brac, lying some seven miles off the mainland port of Split, is the third largest island in the Adriatic. It is some twenty-five miles long and ten miles wide.

[3] For this and other outstanding support to the Yugoslav cause, Tito, some years after the war, decorated both Jack and his brother, Tom, with the Yugoslav Partisan Star.

Painting of KOMIZA, Island of VIS, Yugoslavia by Harold Garland "To the Yugoslav people, in honour of President J B Tito, and his National Liberation Army, from the British Coastal Forces Veterans Association." Presented by Rear Admiral Morgan Giles DSO OBE GM RN on 2nd April 1981.

*Komiza, the port at the Western end of the Island of Vis, was the Headquarters of 2nd Special Service Brigade, commanded by Brigadier Tom Churchill (Jack's brother), and of the Royal Navy Coastal Force units - mostly MGBS, MTBs and MLs. Lieutenant Commander Morgan Giles was the senior Royal Navy officer in Vis- dubbed SNOVIS.*

*The Brigade HQ was set up in March 1944. Jack Churchill had arrived in the Island in January and, with his No.2 Commando group, had already carried out a number of raids on nearby islands, especially against Hvar.*

*The assault on Brac, during which Jack was wounded and captured, was mounted from Komiza, escorted by RN Coastal Force. Angus Sillars, a friend and neighbour of the author, was an officer on board one of the escorting MGBs. While lying offshore during the action they heard Jack's pipes and gathered the assault had failed. When the news came that 'Colonel Jack' had been captured, Coastal Forces hoped it might be able to intercept his transfer to the mainland. However, they were unsuccessful in spotting the small, armed motor launch, in which Jack was carried, during the night of 6th June, from Supetar on the north coast of Brac, eastward to Makarska on the mainland.*

This photograph was taken at HQ 118 Jager Division in the hills near Mostar on the mainland of Yugoslavia on 6th June 1944. Jack had been taken there by launch and car from Brac on the first stage of his journey to Berlin. It was only three days after his capture by the Germans. 'Pops' Manners' blood can still be seen on his left forearm. Jack is holding a battledress blouse, which had belonged to one of his four killed captains - given to him by the Germans, since he was cold.

The helmet he is wearing is from a dead Royal Marine; his own tin hat, covered with a net and with the 2 Commando badge pinned on the front, had been gashed by the splinter which had knocked him out and cut his hand. Jack had dropped off his rank badges and medal ribbons while being escorted to the German HQ, thinking escape might be easier if he said he was of lower rank. However, he decided against it when eleven rank and file, mostly Royal Marines from Y Troop, 40 Commando, joined him.

Wilhelm Heinz is the German officer facing the camera. It was he who sent Jack the photograph and, a Quarter of a century later, arranged his visit to the 1979 Rally of the 118 Jager Division in Austria.

Colonel J.C ('Pops') Manners DSO, who was killed at Jack's side. Under heavy machine gun and mortar fire the main attack failed, Jack lay on the summit with a small group of Royal Marines; he then rolled onto his back and "setting his pipes to his lips played 'Will ye no come back again?'. Finally, stunned by a 'flurry of grenades' he and half-a-dozen other survivors were seized by men of the German 118th Jager. Division[1] which garrisoned the island

Jack - after being taken to Mostar, on the mainland, by motor launch and car - was subsequently interrogated, with firm courtesy, by Major General Keubler, the divisional commander (who could not be persuaded that Jack was not a relation to Winston Churchill), had his sword and pipes confiscated[2], and was flown, by Fieseler Storch and Heinkel III, to Berlin - but not before writing a characteristic 'bread-and-butter' letter to his captors.

In Berlin he was imprisoned in Sachsenhausen concentration camp, being handcuffed and chained to the floor for the first month. His fellow-prisoners included Schuschnigg, the former Chancellor of Austria, Dr. Hjalmar Schacht, the former German Finance Minister, and von Thyssen, the industrialist.

However, not satisfied with prison life, Jack, together with Squadron Leader James[3], a Royal Air Force officer, tunnelled their way under the compound and outer wall of the camp, emerging into the gutter of the road outside and, on 23rd September 1944, set off along the railway towards the Baltic coast. However, in the very dense mist of an early morning, when approaching Rostock, they ran into a work gang which chased them over a high wire fence. Running on they climbed a further barrier, only, having scaled it, to find that it was the internal fence of the workers' camp -and that they were once more 'inside'.

Recaptured, they were later moved south to Niederdorf in Austria, with a group of other prisoners. Ever the opportunist, Jack, on the night of 20th April 1945, when the floodlights failed, walked away, alone, from an outside working party. He continued walking - living on soup made from vegetables gathered from allotments and gardens and cooked in the small, rusty tin which, with onions and matches, he had kept hidden in his jacket for this eventual use - crossing the Alps at the Brenner Pass, keeping wherever possible between the roads and the snowline, with Verona, in Italy, some hundred and fifty miles away, as his objective.

On the eighth day, however, with a sprained ankle and many miles to go, he spotted, on the road far below him, an armoured column, on whose vehicles, to his wild relief and surprise, he could just discern the American white star marking. Running madly, dot-and-carry, down the hillside, he managed to stop one of the last vehicles of the column, a tank. It took some time for the American occupants to credit that this dishevelled scarecrow, dressed in RAF serge uniform, was Colonel Churchill of the British Army. As he told me later, "I couldn't walk very well and was so out of breath I could scarcely talk, but I still managed a credible Sandhurst salute, which may have done the trick".

---

[1] In 1979, Jack and his wife, Rosamund, attended, as guests of honour, the bi-annual rally of the 118th Jager Division at Graz in Austria - a unique distinction and experience.

[2] His claymore and pipes were subsequently exhibited in the South-East Front room in The War Museum in Vienna.

[3] Sqn Ldr 'Jimmie' James MC was one of those recaptured after the 'Great Escape' from Stalag Luft III who was not murdered, but transferred to a concentration camp.

> Nº PI 633 Neresiche
> Brac
> 6 - VI - 44
>
> Dear Captain,
>   Just a short note to thank you & your men, down here, for our correct treatment during our stay with you.
>   The food was rather short, & less than we are used to but that could not be helped under the circumstances.
>   I hope that after the war we shall meet again, & in any case should you at any time find yourself in England or Scotland do ring up HELENSBURGH 2122 or GERRARDS CROSS 2120, where you will find me, & I hope will dine with my wife & I.
>   Farewell.
>                       Jack Churchill

This is Jack's bread-and-butter letter, written in pencil three days after his capture and just before he was despatched to Berlin. The nearest I can get to Jack's 'Neresiche' on a modern map is Nerezisca, a village in the west centre of Brac.

Pt 623 (Jack's Pt 633 and Saunder's Hill 622) marked Visoka, is about three miles due south of Nerezisca on the high ground overlooking the southern shore of the island.

The German officer to whom Jack had given the note was a Hauptman Hans Thorner. Later the note saved Thorner's life when the Yugoslavs wanted to have him shot as a war criminal.

My fifth and final Jack Churchill wartime episode provided me with the Big Laugh.

Shortly after Jack's escape, the war in Europe ended, leaving him with an intense sense of frustration at having missed some of the action and the chance of getting the promotion he had, with good reason, hoped for - command of a Commando Brigade.

"However, there are still the Nips, aren't there?" he was asking his friends.

In the meantime, the 2nd Manchesters (which, by now, I was commanding) were stationed, with most of the 2nd Division, in a remote camp some seventy miles north of Secunderabad in the middle of India, having been flown out of Burma a few weeks previously. It was while we were there - on 18th August 1945 - that everything, thankfully, came to a halt following the fall of the atom bombs on Hiroshima and Nagasaki.

A few days later, to my astonished delight, I got a personal signal from Jack from Bombay, whither, it transpired, he had recently arrived as second-in command of 3 Commando Brigade. 'RV Bombay Yacht Club soonest' it read. Quickly wangling a few days leave, I whipped up to Bombay and, on the evening of my arrival, positioned myself confidently in the bar. Sure enough - eventually - Jack, in the immaculate tropical uniform of a full colonel, splendid with the ribbons of the DSO and bar, and MC, strolled in.

"Jack!!"

"Hullo, Clark!"

It was a great moment and, I seem to remember, we actually shook hands.

"Let's have a drink," said Jack ('Drinking is the Soldier's Pleasure' - `Dryden again). "We've got a long agenda to cover."

As we lifted our first burra pegs, I asked him how he was keeping.

"Fine-o-fine," he replied - and paused; "but you know, Rex, if it hadn't been for those damned Yanks we could have kept the war going for another ten years!"

* * *

To try to sum up, Jack Churchill, though in war a remarkable and inspiring leader, did not always, I believe, appear entirely sympathetic to the average soldier. During the three-week Dunkirk campaign - the first of the war - he was, I know, genuinely surprised and disappointed to discover that all men were not as fearless as he. Perhaps Jack never fully appreciated the earnest desire of the average soldier to live to fight another day, or that the 'squaddie' follows most happily the leader who respects, within the scope of events, this basic sentiment.

Jack once sent me a postcard with the Regimental Colours pictured on it. On the reverse he had written:

*'No Prince or Lord has tomb so proud
as he whose flag becomes his shroud."*

However, as with others of that small, curious band of battlefield genii, this destiny was denied him and, in fact, he survived both the war and subsequent adventures - virtually unscathed -achieved in the main by facing danger calmly and, indeed, with interest, and not by hiding or blindly running away from it.

# PART TWO

*"People are less likely to shoot at you if you smile at them."*

In August 1945, when World War II ended, Jack was rising 39 and just getting into his stride -though hampered by the lack of fighting available. However, there were other avenues to be explored, for one the art of parachuting. So, as a start, at the age of forty, he trained for and gained his 'parachute wings.[1] He also at this time transferred from the Manchesters to the Seaforth Highlanders but, though I told him straight that I considered this to be a retrograde step on his part (to which, I clearly recall, he made no reply), I could, nevertheless, recognize the need he had felt over the years for a deeper association with Scotland - accentuated during the war by commando training in the Highlands.

His first appointment in the Highland Brigade was commanding the demonstration company of the 2nd Seaforths at the School of Infantry at Warminster in Wiltshire. When, in 1948, the 2nd Battalions of all infantry regiments were disbanded, he was appointed second-in-command of the 1st Highland Light Infantry - the old 71st - in Jerusalem.

The situation in Palestine at that time was very delicate. The termination, due in mid-May 1948, of Britain's twenty-five year mandate over the country (set up by the League of Nations after the Great War) and the imminent establishment of the State of Israel, created tensions resulting in widespread acts of terrorism, both by Jewish extremists against the British and between Arab and Jew, especially in and around Jerusalem, the spiritual and political focus of both nations

It was in one of these latter encounters, in Jerusalem, that Jack, again virtually single-handed, offered to rescue a Jewish convoy of doctors, nurses and patients in ambulances (marked with a red Star of David), buses and lorries, ambushed between two mine craters in a narrow street in the Arab quarter of Sheik Jarrah. The convoy was bound for the ultra-modern Hadassah Hospital and the Hebrew University, both situated on Mount Scopus overlooking the Old City - a journey of some two miles from the Jewish road-block at Mea Shearim.

The date was Tuesday, 13th April 1948 - one month and a day before the British Mandate in Palestine was due to expire.

Jack was the first senior officer at the scene of the ambush. He had been on a battalion inspection parade at the 1st Highland Light Infantry's barracks in St. Paul's German Hospice in Jerusalem when he had seen a soldier on the edge of the parade ground wildly waving a piece of paper. Jack, who, as second-in-command, was part of the inspecting party walked over to the soldier, who turned out to be a signals orderly with a wireless message from Tony's post in Sheikh Jarrah.[2] The signal stated that the Jewish Hadassah convoy had been ambushed by the Arabs below the Post, the road had been mined and that much firing was going on. The signal was timed 0930 hours.

---

[1] Jack later commanded the 5th (Scottish) Parachute Battalion: The Only officer to ever command both a Commando and a Parachute regiment.

[2] Tony's Post was a small HLI strongpoint in Sheikh Jarrah. The house belonged to Mrs Katy Antonius - hence its name. It was almost opposite one of the principal Arab strongholds known as The Mufti's House.' (Mrs Antonius may have been related to George Antonius, a Christian Arab and the author of *The Arab Awakening*, an outstanding book on modern Arab nationalists (1939).

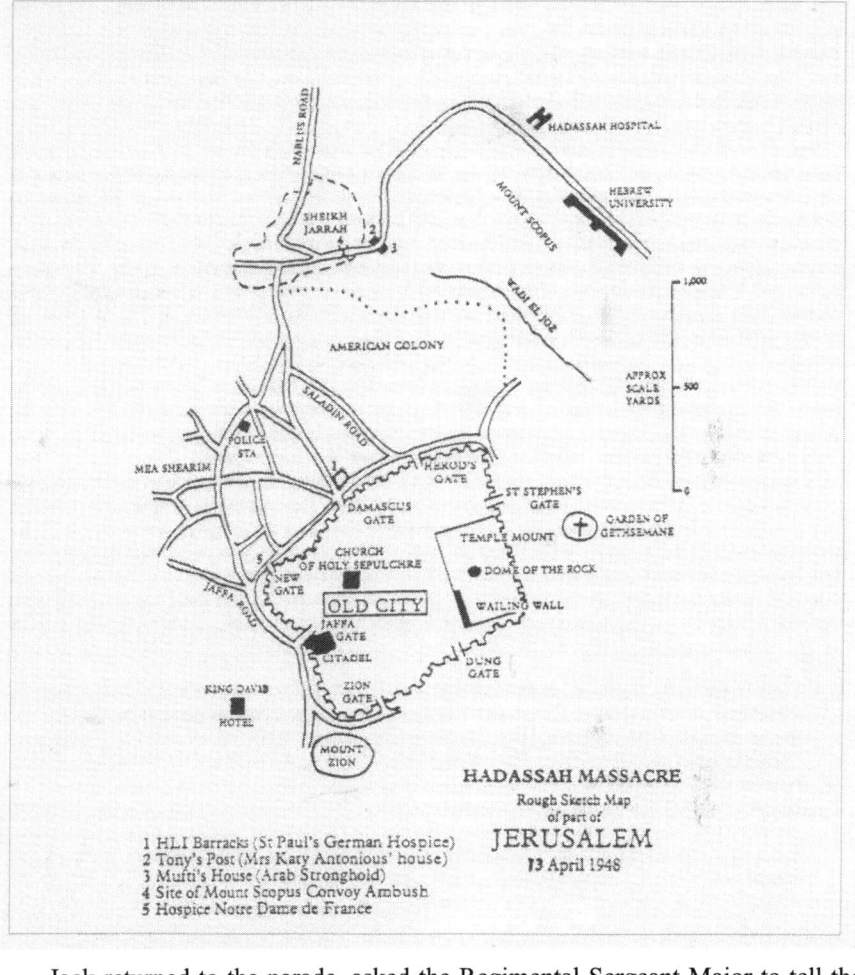

**HADASSAH MASSACRE**
Rough Sketch Map
of part of
**JERUSALEM**
13 April 1948

1 HLI Barracks (St Paul's German Hospice)
2 Tony's Post (Mrs Katy Antonious' house)
3 Mufti's House (Arab Stronghold)
4 Site of Mount Scopus Convoy Ambush
5 Hospice Notre Dame de France

Jack returned to the parade, asked the Regimental Sergeant Major to tell the Commanding Officer, when he got the chance, that there was trouble at Tony's Post and that he, Jack, was going off to see what was happening. Having collected his Dingo[1] and its driver, Jack quickly drove the short mile to Tony's Post, approaching it from the back over a hill using the vehicle's four wheel drive. He then climbed onto the roof of the Post, whence he could look down on the scene of the ambush. This was in full swing about a hundred yards away, with much firing by the Arabs from the houses below on the far side of the road, and to a lesser extent from the Jewish guards in the convoy. Jack also spotted large numbers of Arabs, many armed, swarming up

---

[1] This was a small armoured reconnaissance vehicle, which had been handed into an ordnance depot by the cavalry. Its turret had been removed for repair but it still gave some protection if one kept one's head down. Jack had somehow acquired it for the Battalion for use in 'dicey areas.'

the Wadi el Joz (Valley of the Walnut), below the Arab stronghold of Sheikh Jarrah to join those in the houses.

Jack - the realist - appreciating that "a major Arab/Jewish punch-up" was imminent, at once wirelessed direct to HQ 2nd Infantry Brigade in Jerusalem (the telephone line having been cut by the mine), explained the situation and asked for an artillery observation officer and two 25-pounder field guns to be put at his disposal immediately to blast the Arab gunmen from their ambush positions in the houses. "I need real guns", he said, "not machine guns."

However, Brigade HQ, no doubt startled by such an unorthodox demand and, moreover, desperately anxious at the virtual end of the British Mandate, to steer a middle course between Arab and Jew, turned down his request. Jack, having explained that a very dangerous situation was developing and that some action would have to be taken if the Jews were to be saved, then asked for two Staghounds - large armoured cars with a gun and machine gun - and this was agreed. He was told, however, that it would take some time to get these back from their convoy protection duties elsewhere. "But for Christ's sake try and avoid using their guns," added the staff officer.

"It's only for their cannons I want them," Jack replied.

As there was nothing he could do in the meantime at Tony's Post - which consisted merely of a subaltern officer and about fifteen Jocks with no heavy weapons and only a very limited sortie capacity - but, nevertheless, feeling some responsibility as the man on the spot[1], Jack decided to try to rescue some of the Jews trapped in their buses and lorries by using one of his battalion's big, GMC armoured personnel carriers (APC). Accordingly, having first warned Battalion HQ by wireless to have the vehicles ready, he went back himself in his Dingo to the transport lines and collected an APC with a Bren gun carrier to act as escort. With these two vehicles, and a small police armoured car with a light automatic he picked up on the way back, he returned to the ambush area. On arrival, he positioned the Bren carrier and police armoured car at the Sheikh Jarrah hairpin corner some fifty yards from the trapped convoy, from where they could cover, with their machine guns, the Arab houses and both sides of the road. The APC he placed behind them.

Jack - the romantic now! - then got out of his Dingo and walked about thirty yards, alone, down the road to the Jewish vehicles, in full view of the Arab gunmen in the houses. Later he told me: "As I walked along, swinging my blackthorn walking stick, I grinned like mad from side to side, as people are less likely to shoot at you if you smile at them. Of course, having come straight off a battalion parade, I was very dressed up - in glengarry, tunic, Sam Browne belt (but no claymore, worse luck!) kilt, hair sporran and red and white diced hose - and white spats! This outfit in the middle of the battle, together with my grinning at them, may have made the Arabs laugh because most of them have a sense of humour. Anyway, they didn't shoot me!"

Having arrived at the Jewish buses, he hammered with his blackthorn on the door of the nearest one. A woman's voice called out, "What is that?" Jack replied, "This is Major Churchill of the Highland Light Infantry. I am here with a big, powerful

---

[1] Jack had himself framed the standing orders for HLI strongpoints - on 26th March 1948. These included instructions to prevent fighting between Jews and Arabs as far as possible; if fighting occurred to try to stop it by opening fire on the aggressor; if a Jewish convoy were ambushed by Arabs, to drive off the latter by fire, if possible - but, overall, to avoid at all times exposing British troops to Jew or Arab fire.

armoured vehicle and I can evacuate you from this bus and each of the other buses in turn if you would like to come - but there may be casualties when you transfer from one to the other. Do you understand that?"[1] The woman replied, "Yes, but are you going to drive the Arabs off first?" "No," said Jack. "I cannot do that; I have only twelve men and there are hundreds of Arabs." "Well, I will have to talk to Dr.Yassky[2] or somebody else," said the woman and Jack heard them talking together in Hebrew. After a few moments Jack called out, "Hurry up and decide; it is very dangerous for me outside here." Shortly afterwards the reply came from inside, "Thank you very much but we do not want your help. The Jewish Army - the Haganah - will save us." Jack walked to the other buses repeating his offer and adding that it was their last chance of help from the British and, if they did not accept, it was likely they would all be killed. But in each case the reply was the same - "No thank you; the Haganah will save us."

As he was leaving the buses the HLI Bren carrier driver, who was some seventy-five yards away, shouted out that his Bren gunner, Private Hutton, had been hit and was dying. Jack again shouted to the Jews in the buses: "Look! One of my men has been killed, so I am leaving at once. You are on your own." They called out, "Yes! Yes!" and Jack ran back to his vehicles and sent the APC and the Bren carrier, with the dying soldier, back to the HLI lines. He then went to Tony's Post, which continued to support the trapped vehicles with small arms fire against the Arabs. This fire from Tony's Post and from the small Jewish escort trapped into the convoy for a time prevented the Arabs from directly assaulting the vehicles.

But that was the end of the affair as far as direct intervention in the ambush by the British Army was concerned. Personal help had been offered to the ambushed convoy by Jack Churchill, personifying the Army, and had been refused. The convoy could, in fact, have had, by prior request, a British Army escort, but the Jews had, in recent weeks, become grossly overconfident in their ability to look after themselves - which was, in fact, the root cause of the Sheikh Jarrah tragedy.

After Jack and his vehicles had left the scene, the Arabs, who, by this time, were very numerous in the houses, became emboldened and very noisy, finally setting the Jewish buses on fire with Molotov cocktails and shooting the occupants as they left. By mid-afternoon on 13th April 1948, seventy-seven Jews lay dead. So badly burned and unrecognizable were the bodies from the buses that their remains were buried in a common grave.[3] A further twenty-five Jews were wounded. Only eight of the one hundred and ten men and women who had set out in the Hadassah convoy that Tuesday morning escaped unhurt. When the British armoured cars eventually arrived at 1530 hours they could do little more than survey the carnage. The men of the Highland Light Infantry (which had suffered two killed and three wounded) worked far into the night clearing the bodies, vehicles and debris from the site of the massacre.[4]

---

[1] Jack told me later that he said this to cover himself in case there were subsequent complaints about Jewish casualties.

[2] Dr Chaim Yassky was the Director of Hadassah Hospital and a world-renowned ophthalmologist. He was killed in the ambush. His wife, Fanny, was one of the very few survivors.

[3] A marble monument stands today near the site of the ambush: it lists seventy-six names and one unknown.

[4] *The Palestine Post* of 21st April 1948 quoted a Hadassah staff physiciaan as saying how helpful and considerate British Army assistance was when it arrived.

As the latter half of April went by, sniping and general harassment made life for the Jews on Mount Scopus very difficult, despite the British presence, and a way had to be found to get the seven hundred people down from Hadassah Hospital and the University. Eli Davis, the Deputy Medical Director, asked Jack Churchill for help. Davis's account of his meeting is told in Chapter 15 of Marlin Levin's book, *Balm in Gilead - The Story of Hadassah* as follows:-

"Major Churchill told me there was a slight chance of getting through to Mount Scopus, because the Arabs saw the British meant business. He agreed to make the trip up to Scopus and invited me along. The Major took a Jeep and his driver. I sat, while he stood in the Jeep twirling his stick. He looked as though he were on parade in London. Nothing happened as we went through Sheikh Jarrah. On Scopus we were embraced. We had shown it was possible to get through".

Subsequently, four convoys brought down two hundred patients, a hundred student nurses and three hundred staff members, as well as 600 tons of equipment and supplies. Not a shot was fired. The last convoy, on 5th May, was the biggest because, Davis later claimed, Jack could provide no more help. He had already; he said, exceeded his orders and was in trouble with his superiors.

Finally, a monumental row developed between the British and the Jews over the Hadassah Convoy massacre. Jack Churchill claims that it was his action alone that, in the end, got the Army Command off the hook over what had been, essentially, an Arab/Jewish confrontation. The letter from General Gordon MacMillan, General Officer Commanding British Troops in Palestine, to Dr. J.L. Magnes, President of the Hebrew University, in reply to the Doctor's letters querying the British Army's lack of action during the ambush (reproduced in Appendix A, from the *Palestine Post* of 29th April 1948) would seem to justify Jack's claim to the hilt.

\* \* \*

In 1979, Israel sent a television team to Jack's house in Woking, in Surrey to interview him on the 1948 Hadassah Massacre - an event, especially with the part Jack played in it, still well remembered in Israel. Jack's bold and decisive action on that day in Jerusalem has, however, never been materially recognized by his own country.

In an attempt to be objective over the Army's apparent indecision on 13th April 1948 at Sheikh Jarrah, the allegory occurs to me of a policeman, on his beat, coming upon a street fight. It is his duty to take action to maintain law and order. If the officer is young, enthusiastic and bold, he will doubtless spring to separate the combatants; an older, experienced and more realistic man with an eye, perhaps, on retirement, may well prefer to stand back and pick up the pieces. Could Jack, in this parable, epitomize the former, the Army the latter?

\* \* \*

From Palestine, Jack, in 1953, was posted as an instructor to the School of Land/Air Warfare in Newcastle, north of Sydney in Australia. Here, as well as passing on his special brand of soldiering to Commonwealth soldiers, sailors and airmen, he took up, seriously, the art of surf-riding, designing his own boards and developing a form of hand paddle for getting his run going faster.

When he returned to England in 1954, taking his surfing gear with him, he was appointed as a selector at the War Office Selection Board at Barton Stacey in Hampshire, through which all National Service applicants for commission in the Army had to pass.

From here he planned and subsequently achieved the first-ever surfing run over about a mile and a half of the River Severn's formidable five feet high tidal bore. This achievement was reported in *The Times* and *Evening Standard* of 22nd July 1955. The report was replayed in the Australian Press a few days later, largely as a result of which his feat has been since emulated by some Australian beach surf lifeguards.

The economics of transporting his long[1] narrow board to the Severn from his home in Surrey, some hundred and fifty miles away, much exercised Jack's mind in the planning of the operation. It eventually boiled down to a choice between using Rosamund's "enormously extravagant 25 hp Wolseley" with the board strapped to the roof, or of constructing a trailer to tow behind his motor bike - which by this time was the very Vincent- HRD 'Black Widow' that had won, at record overall and lap speeds, the Senior Clubman's class in the 1952 Isle of Man TT races - as the plate on its tank proclaimed.

Jack finally decided that the latter method would be the thriftier and built himself a tilting trailer for the purpose, which worked well enough. In the event, he was stopped by a policeman in Faringdon on his return journey and charged with towing behind a solo motor-cycle. The subsequent fine was, however, only £2 - "much cheaper", Jack gleefully announced, "than using the 25 hp Wolseley car!"

One of Jack's hobbies - over many years, in fact - was the collection, embellishment and use of radio-controlled scale-model ships - mostly warships - which he turned over from time to time, to advantage, by sales at Christies. The technical standards he had achieved in fitting out and operating these beautiful craft was truly quite remarkable, especially in one who had never been trained in any of the skills required.

In later years Jack's real love, however, lay in full-size steamboats, of which he had owned a bewildering variety and, in which field, he was known as an expert. It was, indeed, a truly fine sight on a summer's day to see an elegant and immaculate steam launch gliding through the waters of the Thames from Richmond to Oxford, its funnel trailing a wisp of smoke, white against the green of the trees of the far bank, with Jack, his steamboat cap square on his head, carrying out the duties of engineer and stoker, while Rosamund at the helm "issues numerous orders," claimed Jack, "blowing the whistle at boats that do not obey the rule of the road and keep to the right."

In 1959, after exactly a third of a century of, on the whole, friendly association with the Army, Jack retired. For the next thirteen years he worked as a 'Retired Officer' (RO), employed as a Civil Servant by the Ministry of Defence as staff officer to the Cadet Force units in London District. This suited him down to the ground, since the job gave him, firstly, an office in the Horse Guards in Whitehall, from which he could look down, with the intense pleasure he had always gained from military ceremonial parades, onto the Household Cavalry mounting guard in the courtyard below, and, secondly, the opportunity of visiting (on his latest motor-bike, perhaps), in their camps, the widespread cadet units in which he took such keen interest.

---

[1] 16-foot - which was very long for those days.

Jack remained the romantic yet realistic individualist, applying to life in general - and war in particular - his inbuilt characteristic of 'unlimited boldness', together with a perpetual zest for living. His unique 'professional amateur' style stemmed originally, I believe, from the 'playing fields' attitude he had eagerly absorbed both at school and, with his two splendid brothers, at home. We could do with more like Jack Churchill - my friend - but, perhaps, not too many more!

\* \* \*

Jack Churchill died peacefully, at St Stephens Hospital, Chertsey on 8th March 1996 aged 89

\* \* \*

*No 2 Commando Officers, Gibraltar 1943*
*(courtesy Commando Veterans Association)*
*Jack Churchill is in the centre of the front row*

# APPENDIX

Extract from *Palestine Post* of 29 April 1948.
The italics are the author's:
"The full text has now been published of the correspondence between *Dr J. L. Magnes, President of the Hebrew University and Chairman of the Hadassah Council in Palestine, and General MacMillan, the GOC* concerning the killing of 76 Jews in the Hadassah convoy trapped in Sheikh Jarrah for about seven hours on 13 April. *It is stated in a letter dated 23 April, ten days after the event, that an attempt was made to bring help within an hour and a half of the attack, when a courageous officer of the Highland Infantry backed a lone vehicle up to the convoys and offered to rescue as many as he could take* and that this "offer was not accepted". There appear to be no survivors among those to whom he spoke, as nobody was up to now aware that this effort had been made.

The GOC adds that he resented the suggestion that nothing had been done until late afternoon, as he himself had passed the scene of the attack at 9.45 and had judged the situation to be clearing up. He had been surprised to find heavy firing still in progress at 4.30, when he returned by the same route.

There is also a protest by the Arab Higher Committee that the Army should have intervened to rescue the survivors.

The correspondence, as issued by the Public Information Office on Tuesday, follows:

**Dr J.L. Magnes to Brigadier C.F. Jones (OBE, MC Commander, 2nd Infantry Brigade):**

I am sending you herewith a copy of some notes prepared by Dr J.M. Bromberg, one of the trusted physicians of the Hadassah Hospital, concerning what took place in the ambulance in which Dr Yassky, the Director of the Hospital, was killed. (These were published in *The Palestine Post* on 21 April.)

You will see that Dr Yassky received his fatal wound at 2.30pm.

I telephoned you at 1.45 that day asking if it was not possible to send vehicles to rescue those who had been trapped since 9.45 that morning. You said that that was what you were trying to do, but the difficulty was that a major battle was going on.

I have tried to explain to myself and to others why this should have prevented the rescue of those valuable lives whose passing we are now mourning. I confess, I am not able to explain it. This is the reason why I am writing you this letter and *why I am sending copies to the High Commissioner, The GOC* [General MacMillan] and the Chief of Staff.

I am not without a sense of guilt myself. Perhaps had I made my appeal to you stronger at 1.45, my friend and fellow-worker, Dr Yassky, would not have been killed at 2.30, and the other teachers and laboratory workers of the University might have had their lives spared.

As you know, I have been very grateful for the efforts you have made during the past several weeks to keep the road to the Hospital open and comparatively secure. I cannot, however, rid myself of the fateful question: Why was it not possible to rescue men and women bent on errands of mercy and of science between the hours of 9.45 in the morning and the hours of the late afternoon?

*15 April 1948*

**General MacMillan to Dr Magnes**
Thank you for your further letter of 18 April regarding the events of 13 April at Sheikh Jarrah.

The answer to your question is simple. When the firing at the immobilized Jewish vehicles became heavy *the second-in-command of the HLI succeeded in himself backing a British armoured vehicle up to the stranded Jewish vehicles. At considerable personal risk he got out and attempted to persuade the Jews to get out of their own vehicle and get into the British one. This they refused to do. They insisted on remaining in their own vehicles. The Officer could not remain there indefinitely under fire. Persuasion having failed there was no other course open to him than to come away again. This occurred at 11.15 am.*

I hope you will agree, therefore, *that a very definite and indeed gallant effort was made to rescue these unfortunate persons.* The fact that the effort failed was wholly caused by their refusal to be evacuated from their own vehicles.

My impression is that in the persistent propaganda against the British troops *this brave action on the part of my officer and the suicidal attitude of the occupants of the Jewish vehicles have been deliberately ignored* and the sooner it is made public the better.

*23 April 1948*

Letters omitted: General MacMillan to Dr Magnes of 15 April 1948 and Dr Magnes to General MacMillan of 18 April 1948."

# POST SCRIPTS

Victoria Cross Recommendation  57

Daily Telegraph Obituary  58

# VICTORIA CROSS RECOMMENDATION

Jack's recommendation for a VC (*p.40*) was a well known fact in No 2 Commando Brigade as evidenced by two reliable sources:

**Major General Tom Churchill** was Jack's elder brother. He was also in the Commando Brigade and knew Brigadier Laycock - Jack's superior officer and Brigade commander at the Salerno Landing - personally from his position as the Brigadier's right hand man. It can therefore be assumed that he would only have included the following facts in his family history *The Churchill Chronicles* if they were indisputable and, as there was a degree of friendly competition between the two brothers, Tom would never have given his brother this accolade if it was not true to his certain knowledge.

"The island of Sicily was captured in three months, and an expeditionary force under General Bernard Montgomery was organised to invade Italy as quickly as possible. The Commando Brigade on the island was joined by No. 2 Commando from Gibraltar, whose commanding officer was now Lieut. Colonel Jack Churchill. This force carried out a landing in the south west of Italy at Salerno, in September 1943, and Jack and Tom Churchill were together again in action, the latter now second in command to Brigadier Laycock, who commanded the brigade.

A fierce battle resulted, in the course of which No. 2 Commando bore the brunt of the fighting, and Jack Churchill was recommended for the Victoria Cross, though ultimately he was awarded only the D.S.O. By this time he had acquired the sobriquet of 'Mad Jack'* as a result of his many exploits, a nickname which, strangely, an ancestor, Joseph, had earned about a century and a half earlier."

*No doubt why Rex King-Clark included the Dryden quotation reproduced on page 33 in this book.

**Lieutenant Bob Bishop MC** served as an NCO under Jack. Writing on the Commando Corps Veterans' website http://www.commandoveterans.org some 63 years later he says:

"There is that matter of a decoration. At Salerno Jack and his runner had operated far out ahead of the Commando and entered the enemy-held village of Pigoletti, whereupon Jack descended on each German sentry post or weapons pit, made its occupants prisoner and delivered them group by group to be guarded by the waiting runner. When the count was made it amounted to 42 prisoners Jack had taken. He even made the German mortar crews carry out their own mortars. The prisoners with all their weapons were then handed over to the leading Commando troop when it finally caught up with Jack. For this audacious feat of arms Col. Jack was recommended for the Victoria Cross, which was in due course watered down to a D.S.O. Why? The award of the V.C. had certainly been made as a result of actions concerning far-lesser valour."

# DAILY TELEGRAPH OBITUARY
## 13 March 1996

**Lieutenant-Colonel Jack Churchill, who has died aged 89, was probably the most dramatically impressive Commando leader of the Second World War.**

His exploits - charging up beaches dressed only in a kilt *(see footnote)* and brandishing a dirk, killing with a bow and arrow, playing the bagpipes at moments of extreme peril - and his legendary escapes won him the admiration and devotion of those under his command, who nicknamed him "Mad Jack".

Churchill believed an assault leader should have a reputation which would at once demoralise the enemy and convince his own men that nothing was impossible. He was awarded two DSOs and an MC, and mentioned in despatches.

Romantic and sensitive, he was an avid reader of history and poetry, knowledgeable about castles and trees, and compassionate to animals, even to insects.

John Malcolm Thorpe Fleming Churchill was born in Surrey on Sept 16 1906. His father, Alex Churchill, was on leave from the Far East, where he was Director of Public Works in Hong Kong and Ceylon.

After education at the Dragon School, Oxford, King William's College, Isle of Man, and Sandhurst, Churchill was commissioned in 1926 into the Manchester Regiment and gazetted to the 2nd Battalion, which he joined in Rangoon.

Returning from a signals course at Poona, he rode a Zenith motor-cycle 1,500 miles across India, at one point crashing into a water buffalo. In Burma, he took the Zenith over railway bridges by stepping on the sleepers (there was nothing in between them) and pushing the bike along the rails.

Churchill moved from Rangoon to Maymyo where he was engaged in "flag marches", which meant moving up and down the Irrawaddy by boat, visiting the villages and deterring those who might be contemplating robbery, murder or dacoity.

At Maymyo he learned to play the bagpipes, tutored by the Pipe Major of the Cameron Highlanders, and became an oustanding performer. But when the regiment returned to Britain in 1936, he became bored with military life at the depot at Ashton-under-Lyne and retired after only 10 years in the Army.

Churchill went on a grand tour of Europe, accompanied by his great friend Rex King-Clark; took minor parts as an archer in films; played the bagpipes as an entertainer; and represented Great Britain at archery in the 1939 World Championships.

On the outbreak of war in 1939, he was recalled to the Colours and went to France, taking with him his bow and arrows which he used on patrols against the Germans in front of the Maginot Line. The weapon was silent, accurate to 200 yards and lethal.

After the Germans attacked in France, Churchill was awarded the MC in the retreat at the Battle of l'Epinette (near Bethune) where his company was trapped by German forces.

Churchill fought back with two machine guns (and his bow) until ammunition was exhausted, then extricated the remains of the company through the German lines at night and reported back to Brigade HQ. Later he was wounded and carried a bullet in his shoulder all his life.

After returning to England, he joined the Commandos and in 1941 was second-in-command of a mixed force from 2 and 3 Commandos which raided Vaagso, in Norway. The aim was to blow up local fish oil factories, sink shipping, gather intelligence, eliminate the garrison and bring home volunteers for the Free Norwegian Forces.

Before landing, Churchill decided to look the part. He wore silver buttons he had acquired in France; carried his bow and arrows and armed himself with a broad-hilted claymore; and led the landing force ashore with his bagpipes. Although he was again wounded, the operation forced the Germans to concentrate large forces in the area.

After recovering, Churchill was appointed Lieutenant-Colonel commanding No 2 Commando which he took through Sicily (leading with his bagpipes to Messina) and then to the landings at Salerno.

They captured the village of Pigoletti and its garrison of 42 men as well as an 81 mm mortar and its crew. In further fighting along the Pigoletti Ridge, he was recommended for the VC but eventually received the DSO. His action had saved the Salerno beachhead at a critical time.

Churchill's next assignment was in the Adriatic, where he was appointed to command a force comprising No 43 Royal Marine Commando plus one company from the Highland Light Infantry and eight 25 lb guns.

They landed on the island of Brac, then attacked and captured the Vidova Gora (2,500 ft high), the approaches of which were heavily mined. Playing his pipes, Churchill led No 40 Commando in a night attack which reached the top of the objective where he was wounded and captured.

"You have treated us well," he wrote to the German commander after only 48 hours in captivity. "If, after the war, you are ever in England and Scotland, come and have dinner with my wife and myself"; he added his telephone number. The German was one Captain Hans Thornerr and later that note saved Thornerr's life when the Yugoslavs wanted to have him shot as a war criminal.

The Germans thought, wrongly, that Churchill must be a relation of the Prime Minister. Eventually he was imprisoned in Sachsenhausen Camp, near Berlin, where he was chained to the floor for the first month and found himself in company with such VIPs as Kurt von Schusnigg, the former Chancellor of Austria, von Thyssen, and Schacht, the former German Economics Minister.

Churchill tunnelled out of the camp with an RAF officer, but was recaptured and transferred to a PoW camp in Austria. When the floodlights failed one night he escaped and, living on stolen vegetables, walked across the Alps near the Brenner Pass. He then made contact with an American reconnaissance column in the Po Valley.

Churchill was appointed second-in-command of No 3 Commando Brigade, which was in India preparing for the invasion of Japan, but the war ended - much to his regret, as he wanted to be killed in battle and buried in the Union flag.

He took a parachute course, making his first jump on his 40th birthday, and commanded 5th (Scottish) Parachute Battalion, thus becoming the only officer to command both a Commando and a Parachute battalion.

Churchill had always wanted to serve with a Scottish regiment, and so transferred to the Seaforth Highlanders, becoming a company commander.

In 1948 he was appointed second-in-command of the Highland Light Infantry, then serving in Jerusalem. Terrorism was widespread and on April 13 1948, Arabs ambushed a Jewish convoy of doctors en route for the Hadassah Hospital, near Jerusalem.

Churchill, having ordered reinforcements for his small force, walked alone towards the ambush, smiling and carrying a blackthorn stick. "People are less likely to shoot you if you smile at them," he said. So it proved.

He then managed to evacuate some of the Jews but they thought that Haganah (the Jewish army) would save them and did not require his services. As one of the HLI had now been killed by Arab fire, he withdrew; 77 Jews were then slaughtered. Later Churchill assisted in the evacuation of 500 patients and staff from the hospital.

Back in Britain, he was for two years second-in-command of the Army Apprentices School at Chepstow before serving a two-year stint as Chief Instructor, Land/Air Warfare School in Australia.

In 1954, Churchill joined the War Office Selection Board at Barton Stacey. During this period he rode a surf board a mile and a half up river on the Severn bore.

His last post was as First Commandant of the Outward Bound School.

After retirement, Churchill devoted himself to his hobby of buying and refurbishing steamboats on the Thames; he acquired 11, which made journeys from Richmond to Oxford. He was also a keen maker of radio-controlled model boats, which he sold at a profit. He also took part in motor-cycling speed trials.

When not engaged in military operations Jack Churchill was a quiet, unassuming man, though not above astonishing strangers for the fun of it. In his last job he would sometimes stand up on a train journey from London to his home, open the window and hurl out his briefcase, then calmly resume his seat. Fellow passengers looked on aghast, unaware that he had flung the briefcase into his own back garden.

Jack Churchill married, in 1941, Rosamund Denny; they had two sons.

**Footnote:** Henry Brown OBE, National Secretary of the Commando Association, writing in the Commando Association Newsletter No 103 dated Sept 1996, commented:

"The National Press obituary notices outlined in great detail the sterling qualities of Colonel Jack, describing him rightly as probably the most dramatically impressive Commando leader of the Second World War. One could go to great lengths in describing his charm and countless attributes, and doubtless, all comrades privileged to know him closely, especially those in No.2 Commando, know how daring and fearless he was; certainly 'a man born to lead'. Not surprisingly, he soldiered on after the war and in spite of his many varied interests and activities he always took a very close interest in our Association and we look back with much pleasure on his two periods, 1957-8 and 1968-70, as our President.

For his dear widow Rosamund, we correct the following inaccuracies in the Daily Telegraph obituary notice. Colonel Jack, always particular about being correctly dressed, did not transfer to the Seaforth Highlanders until after the war. Neither did he rush up any beaches "dressed only in a kilt", nor was he born in Surrey, but Sri Lanka."